Praise for
Business Model

"Williams is an innovator, mentor, speaker, and champion for diversity and inclusion; an avid believer in reaching back and uplifting others."

—*Black Enterprise Magazine*

"David is one of the most incredible leaders I have [ever] met. For all of his technology genius and innovation, he keeps it real for all people to see. He leads with love, kindness, and a will to share with others. His passion is to change the world with his skill and willingness to take others up with him."

—Nancy Leiberman,
Broadcaster for ABC, NBC, ESPN,
Basketball Hall of Famer,
and Olympic Silver Medalist

"David is smart, inquisitive, and an innovator. He drives for success and what is best."

—Andy Geisse,
Former CEO of AT&T Business Solutions

"David's remarkable story should inspire others to follow their dreams. He is a role model for how to overcome adversity and live without limits.

—Ralph de la Vega,
Former Vice Chairman of AT&T and
CEO of Business Solutions International

"David has a unique ability to identify high-value transformative opportunities to create success through automation. Leading a culturally diverse team of developers, he has been a great motivator and brings out the best in each team member."

—Vedant Jhaver,
CEO of Prodapt

"David's leadership, courage, humility, and undeniable orientation toward cooperation are a testament to his unique ability to positively influence and inspire people to work towards a shared and valuable goal for the organization. David employs a natural level of emotional intelligence. I've witnessed his ability to manage his emotions and the emotions of others to diffuse tense situations and turn potential foes of the project into champions."

—Michael Oiknine,
CEO of CallVU Inc.

Business Model

When Incredible Will meets Professional Skill

David C. Williams

Made for Success Publishing
P.O. Box 1775 Issaquah, WA 98027
www.MadeForSuccessPublishing.com

Distributed by Made for Success Publishing

First Printing

Library of Congress Cataloging-in-Publication data

Williams, David C.
    Business Model: When Incredible Will Meets Professional Skill

        p. cm.

LCCN: 2022908616
ISBN: 978-1-64146-387-4 *(HDBK)*
ISBN: 978-1-64146-394-2 *(eBOOK)*
ISBN: 978-1-64146-497-0 *(AUDIO)*

Printed in the United States of America

For further information contact Made for Success Publishing
+14255266480 or email service@madeforsuccess.net

Contents

A Rudolph Moment

IN ORGANIZING MY THOUGHTS throughout these pages, I've contemplated the breadth and depth of experiences, stories, relationships, hardships, and triumphs. Today, as I write this, I'm trying not to get too wound up in the seriousness of my first book and the pressures that come from that. In fact, I'm thinking I just want to have fun. There are some pretty dark moments I'll discuss later, but after you've been through as many as I have, you learn to force the fun in wherever you can. And with that...

At this very moment, I'm listening to all three versions of "Rudolph the Red-Nosed Reindeer" on repeat. The version by Gene Autry and Johnny Marks, the version by The Temptations, and the version by DMX. When listening to these different adaptations, I struggle with deciding if there is one better than the other. One cannot deny the absolute genius of Gene Autry and Johnny Marks to craft such a story that would last throughout the ages. However, The Temptations are arguably the soul and harmony of humanity. It's spectacular to hear how they reshape a children's song and create such a rhythmic rendition that would force even the most serious to sing or sway. But the passion of DMX is undeniable and infectious, and you can hear the heart of a man who has seen so much find incredible joy in a Christmas song.

And, yes, there's one inspiring golden thread through them all: the fact that all Rudolph needed was one foggy night, and Christmas would never be the same. *Ever!* What started as Santa's crisis and Rudolph's toxic environment later became a household holiday theme. Even when it was rough, Rudolph never gave up.

I'd like to propose that each one of us is just one opportunity away from our Rudolph moment. We just need to be ready when it comes along. Don't get me wrong; I'm sure Rudolph had some tough days and rough nights. I'm sure he needed some motivation from some elder Reindeer that believed he was truly special. Hopefully, there were some mentors before him that really wanted to see him ascend higher than themselves. They probably told Rudolph where to be and when to be there. And while the darkness swallowed the night and the fog descended upon Rudolph's destiny, he embraced the reins of opportunity and held on for dear life as he rose above his circumstance like a bouquet of flowers. The truth is, nearly everyone who is at the top of their field started off as Rudolph: gifted beyond comprehension but undervalued.

This is why we must recall and draw from the triumphs and learnings of our past experiences. You are just one foggy night from achieving everything you ever wanted. Are you ready? It might cost you more than you expected. Rudolph's cost included new work hours, missing sleep hours, and frequent flyer miles. Not being deeply rooted in our passion, whatever that cost might be, could sway us to give up when the price for our goal increases beyond our budget of belief. Unwavering passion is immensely valuable, and a much-needed resource on the journey for excellence.

Do you have a support system that will pay the bill when your emotional account is depleted? Friends and family members who speak positivity into you are priceless. Reciprocating that support is a great way to show thanks. Unfortunately, everyone does not have an immediate support system. For those who do not have someone they can lean on, don't give up. Your support system is on its way. Your story is different, your support system will be different, and how they support you will look different than anyone else's. There are countless examples of those who were counted out and wound up making it *all* count.

In fact, I find that being counted out is a catalyst for making opportunities count the most when it's your moment. In a mathematical sense, the thing that people usually don't count on is the anomaly. It's easy to get caught up in thinking, "99.99% of the time, _____ (fill in the blank)." However, every now and then, those unbeatable odds defy logic. When we are defining our future, the journey will have many unexpected lessons that will be needed to reach our professional goals. At every turn, we must believe we are the unbeatable odd. We are the anomaly to the formula of life. We, anomalies, are the exceptions defining new rules.

When I look back at my past experiences, there are countless times I've had to overcome hardships, disappointments, or being misjudged. I have come to understand this is the process of the anomaly's journey in realizing that we are the exception to the rule. The hardships of life didn't take us out. We have the gift of experience from being on the survived, triumphed, or victorious side of that hardship. These experiences usually bring something special out of us. Sometimes it's something profound, sometimes it's something subtle. Regardless of how large of an impact each experience is, they are all needed to reach and sustain the larger goal. This process of overcoming is how our own unique business model is shaped. It's the practice we need to perfect our talents and skills. So, when the going gets tough, stay focused.

There's no shortcut to our greatness. The very best things in life are on the other side of fear. They are there so that they are protected from others and also protected from ourselves. But when we have the courage and faith to overcome, those doors open. Jesus didn't "want" someone at his own table betraying Him any more than Tony Stark wanted Captain America to choose the Winter Soldier over Iron Man. The point is, life deals the very best of the best a cold hand at times. Recognizing our foggy night, being prepared for life-changing moments, and exercising our faith in the moment is what progresses us. These moments give us the opportunity to have an insightful experience in which our passion is needed to overcome. This combination of passion and past experiences creates a tailor-made unique business model for success.

Life deals the very best
of the best a cold hand at times.

It's what you do with that hand that defines you.

Mama, I'll Be...

SOME DATES NEVER LEAVE YOU. Like August 22, 1983. It was a Saturday.

It was two months after my eighth birthday, and my mother was in the kitchen preparing a meal for my sister Angelia Loria and me. Angelia, who was 13 years old at the time, was in her room while I was playing around with my skateboard.

I would usually ride on the sidewalk, but on this day, I was just rolling around inside. One knee rested on the skateboard while the other foot pushed me. At the time, I was making my rounds. I toured through our home, starting in the living room. I pushed down the hall through the kitchen and back into the living room again.

As I rolled into the living room, I peered through the large-pane glass window and noticed my father's beautiful Cadillac Eldorado parked in the driveway. I could see him on the porch, just about to reach the front door. Something was different. He was stuffing a pistol in his back pocket.

When he came inside, he rushed into my mother's room carrying a manila folder. He started talking about what happens after death, like Social Security for the kids. I didn't quite understand what was going on, but I knew it was serious. Sensing that it wasn't good, I decided to go find my sister.

Just as I ran down the hall and into her room, my sister noticed the commotion in the other room. "Uh, I think we should call 911, Chris. We need to go to the neighbor's house."

Note: My dad's name is David. So, when I was born, my family called me by my middle name, Chris(topher).

Angelia had always been incredibly perceptive. Even as a young teenager, she knew we should call for help from a neighbor's phone instead of our own.

While we were trying to figure out what we were going to do, my father left the room and walked through the kitchen into the dining room. Following him, my mother attempted to reason with him. She was desperately trying to de-escalate the situation. Just as they were moving through the kitchen, my sister grabbed me by the hand.

"Come on, Chris," she said, pulling me out of her room. We ran through my mother's room and out into the backyard. She was leading us next door to Mrs. Mitchell's home.

In that space between our homes, I heard the sound. *Bang! Bang!*

Two distinct, deafening firearm blasts. The first thing that came to mind was the absolute worst—the sound of losing both parents. My sister, my hero, didn't stop. She continued to move quickly and get us to the neighbor's house. Once we reached Mrs. Mitchell, my sister asked her to call the police and an ambulance.

Mrs. Mitchell called the authorities and accompanied my sister and me as we ran back to our home and through the front door. My mother was in the living room sitting on a cabinet-style, old-school record player. The kind that's made of wood and has a hinged top panel that opens from the top. She was crying profusely.

A few neighbors came over, and I remember half a dozen people on our front porch asking if everything was all right.

The paramedics arrived along with the police, and our home was suddenly very busy. There were a lot of people; a lot of commotion, and a lot of emotion. We were all in shock. My mother was crying uncontrollably, and I remember saying five words to her. Five words that have been a North Star for me my entire life. I begged my mother not to cry and then said those five words, "Mama, I'll be the man."

At 8 years old, I didn't quite know what I was saying. But over the years, I've never shied away from the role or the work, no matter how difficult the situation.

Through all the commotion, I wanted to be with my mother, but they asked Angelia and me to give our mom some time and wait in my sister's room. So, we did.

Relatives from my mother's side of the family started showing up and tried to provide comfort and consolation. From my sister's window, I saw the paramedics wheel my father down the porch steps on a stretcher; his head was completely bandaged as if he were wearing a white nightcap with a red stain.

On the day of the incident, my father was not pronounced dead. He was sustained via life support for three days, and my mother, sister, and I visited him each day he was there. I tried talking to him, but he was unresponsive. I overheard one of the hospital staff use the term "vegetable."

I remember being at home and receiving the phone call that he had passed away. It hit us all like a ton of bricks. My father was everything to us—he was a veteran and a family man.

I am the youngest of six siblings: Victor, Andrea, David Jr., Orlando, and Angelia. My father insisted that we all have a very tight relationship with each other. We never saw each other as and sisters. If someone asked, the response was always the same: "that's my brother" or "that's my sister." That's all we've ever known.

My father used to coordinate large family reunion trips to the beach. I remember several trips to Galveston where there would be seven or eight vehicles traveling together. My father and my Uncle Herman would go back and forth on the CB radio using their radio handles. Uncle Herman had a lighter complexion, and his CB handle name was

Snowman. My father was six-foot-one and lean, so his handle name was Thin Man.

As a little boy, it was such a joy to hear them: [squelch, squelch] "Breaker, breaker one-nine. Snowman, this is Thin Man headed southbound on I-45. Gotta gator in hammer lane and local yokel on the hill. Come back, over."

My father was the kind of guy who would go on hunting trips and come back with big game, and he would use a BB gun to kill a squirrel before actually preparing the meat and cooking it. He was also fearless. He had skydived and served in the military in the early 60s, around the time of the Berlin conflict.

As a young child, I personally remember being with my father when he would counsel suicide survivors. I remember one man who had attempted to commit suicide by putting a shotgun in his mouth and pulling the trigger. That man lived in Dixon Circle, a very rough part of the city. I specifically remember my father breaking up a fight between two other men. He and I were in the car, and he pulled over and stopped. With his words *and* his will, he convinced the two men to go their separate ways.

My father was gifted. I remember the days when I would come home from school to find that he had drawn me a scene from a cartoon just by watching the television. Every weekend, he carried me to the nearby K-Mart to go buy a toy—as long as I was being responsible in school. However, he also challenged my intellect by actively encouraging me to read more books each week. Before he passed, I was up to about 13 books a week.

He made sure that all his children felt his love; my father was intentional and consistent about it. My sister Angelia was a daddy's girl. He was her hero. He made it a point to teach us to fish, casting our lines from the bank with cane poles and occasionally from Uncle Herman's boat. He taught us all to drive. At a young age, he sat me in his lap and let me control the steering wheel while he worked the pedals and taught me to drive.

Lastly, my father was an active member of the church. Not a deacon or preacher, but he was a working hand for the Lord.

So, at least for me, this notion of him taking his life just seemed out of the blue. As I got older, however, I put a few of the pieces together and started to realize there were a few things that may have contributed to his skewed perspective in believing taking his life would solve anything. My mother and father divorced, which was likely stressful. He also began to date someone who was using narcotics, and he began to do so as well.

Not once did my mother ever utter one negative thing about my dad. And, although I hated that he was gone, I never resented him. There were times during my adolescence when I knew I needed him. I knew he had the answers to the issues I was going through. If I could just get a little bit of time with him, he would know exactly what

I needed to do: whether dealing with matters of the heart or fake friends. The kind of people who act like they're in your corner, but when it's time to reciprocate, will not go the extra mile for you. I can remember times when one or more of these frenemies got a little too close to me for a little too long. My dad would have helped me recognize that.

Unfortunately, this would not be my future, for my father was gone.

Soon after his passing, a rift opened in the family, and some of them blamed my mother. It was a long time before my siblings and I started hanging out on a consistent basis again.

I learned several things from this tragic series of events. I learned that if I had a child, I would never leave him or her—*ever*. I learned that my sister was amazing at crisis management, staying calm, and knowing the right next step to get through tough times. All things considered, it was a blessing for my big sister to take charge and know what to do. She is my hero. I also learned how devoted my mother was (and is) to making family work.

My mom never remarried, and it took a long time before I could fully understand why. I asked her once, and she said, "When you've had top shelf, the rest just won't do."

"When you've had top shelf,
the rest just won't do."

The Candy Marketplace

I WAS IN BETWEEN THE SECOND AND THIRD GRADE when my father committed suicide. As I mentioned earlier, it was August, just before school started. The first day of school was never the same for me after that. The next year was a complete blur as I finished the third grade at Charles Rice Elementary School. In the following year, my mother tried something audacious. She attempted to give me a chance at a better education and enrolled me in Saint Anthony Catholic School.

Currently, Saint Anthony is an excellent charter school with accolades to substantiate. That said, at the time, Saint Anthony was the poorest Catholic school in Dallas. Period. And no one needed a financial analysis or balance sheet to figure that out. There was one school bus. It was green and barely worked, but the students had no issue with that because no one wanted to ride it!

Don't get me wrong: Saint Anthony is an amazing school. I have nothing but great memories from my time there. (Well, maybe there was one downside, but we'll get to that later.) Great memories like watching Michael Jordan play basketball, and during school one year we watched the space shuttle launch. I also learned the beauty of diversity at Saint Anthony. My gym teacher was a man from Africa who not only taught us the importance of physical fitness but also helped us to understand and appreciate cultures very far from our immediate surroundings and neighborhoods.

One of my favorite teachers, Ms. Gray, left a lasting impression on me. She was the kind of person who had a quote for everything. One of my favorite quotes was "Excuses, excuses. The road to failure is paved with excuses."

I fell in love with music while attending Saint Anthony. I learned to play the recorder and the saxophone, as well as harmonic songs of worship that are sung a cappella and in layers. And, of course, I learned the Bible at Saint Anthony. We had lots of learning exercises, including games for memorizing all the books of the Bible and discussions that would bring the people and stories to life instead of just reading through a historical account.

My love for organized sports also started at Saint Anthony. Though our football team was small, with a total of 13 players from fourth to eighth grade, God blessed us. (For reference, most teams have around 53 players.) In 1986, we went to the District Championship. For those who are not familiar with the game of football, it requires at least 11 players to be on the field (from each team) to play the game. So, if the home team is on offense, they are then required to have 11 players on the field, and the visiting team would also have 11 defensive players on the field. And when possession of the ball changes, each team would again have to put 11 players on the field to oppose each other. That means that most of our team was on the field *at all times*. Therefore, you start to see what kind of students Saint Anthony was comprised of.

But wait, there's more! Saint Anthony is a small school, with just one classroom of students per grade level. Oh, and we didn't have a practice field. When it was time for practice, we would suit up in our football gear and walk half a mile to Exline Recreational Center. The rec center didn't have a football field, so we just found an empty grassy area to hold practice. The type of football practice we had then—bullpen exercises, for those familiar with the sport—are no longer allowed today. Through all of this, the coaches taught us to be tough and resilient. "Teamwork makes the dream work" was the motto.

Our coaches taught us the fundamentals the best they could. However, looking back, it felt more like the Spartan 300, where the total is greater than the sum of the parts (and sometimes doesn't even make logical sense). We counted on one another, and the bond between us was the source of our strength. After an hour or more of practice, we would walk back to the school and load our football gear in our parents' car, or we would carry it by hand and walk home, looking forward to the next practice.

This isn't a sports book, so I'll sum up the season as quickly as I can. We played some strong teams; we didn't win all the games, but we won most of them. We learned how to lose, and we learned how to win. We learned how to deal with defeat and how not to lose our minds when we were successful. We learned balance. Yes, most of the teams we played were predominantly white, and we dealt with racism. However, it mostly stemmed from the opposing team's parents, and only on occasion from other students or coaches. We all had dealt with racism before, so no one ever panicked. We just took our win and went on. And on. And on.

Until we went to the Diocese District Championship. We lost that game. The other team had 53 players, and they were all very well-conditioned. They looked like giants, but they won fair and square. Lastly, each team member learned to play offense, defense, kick-off, kick-off return, punt, and punt-return. No one ever complained. No one. Ever. No, really, *ever.*

In addition to sports and music, I also learned business while attending Saint Anthony. For me to attend, my mother had to pay tuition. At the time, the tuition was $140 a month. In order to afford the school, my mother, who worked at the United States Post Office, had to work overtime. To accomplish putting in 10 to 12 hours a day and still get me to school on time, a routine had to be established and strictly followed.

At this time, my father was a year deceased. We had recently moved from South Dallas to Pleasant Grove, and we used my grandmother's home address so that I would be within the location for Saint Anthony. She was my mom's mother. Though her full name was Beatrice Alice Wyatt, she was commonly known as Big Mama to all 19 of the grandchildren.

A typical school day would start like this:

- My mother would wake me at 5:00 in the morning.
- We would leave home by 5:30.
- We would get to Big Mama's house by 5:45.
- Mom would start work by 6:00.
- It was still dark outside, so I would sleep on Big Mama's couch until 7:00.
- I would walk to the bus stop a couple blocks away to catch the 7:15 bus.

The 7:15 bus was on the 44 Oakland line. For those who have ridden city buses as a primary means of transportation, you'll know what I mean when I say the 44 Oakland bus line was tough. It went to Bonton, which was the roughest part of the city. There were a couple other corners of Dallas that were as notorious, including Dixon Circle (also South Dallas) and Fish Trap Road (West Dallas projects).

The street that leads to Bonton crosses a floodgate and dead-ends at a levee (talk about a trap) where a large complex of projects existed. The name of this street is Bexar Street, which is, believe it or not, pronounced "Bear" Street. After leaving Big Mama's house, I would walk to Bexar Street to catch the bus to Saint Anthony. The actual bus stop was on the corner of Bexar Street and Macon Street, where the ever-popular Val's Liquor Store was found. It was right in the heart of South Dallas.

Val was a man who was well-respected in the neighborhood—and maybe a little feared, too. He was known as a person who was not to be messed with, and no one tried him. Or at least, there were no *stories* of anyone trying him. That said, Val was always nice to the kids.

Nowadays, it's hard to imagine a liquor store being open that early in Texas. Currently, Texas liquor laws won't allow stores to open before 10 a.m. on weekdays. Needless to say, it was a different era of life back then. Almost every morning, around 7:10, I would wait for the bus inside Val's Liquor Store. Often, he and I were the only people in the store.

Because my mom would work overtime in the evenings, I would go to Big Mama's house to wait for her after school. My mom worked in South Dallas at the Juanita Craft Post Office, which wasn't very far from Big Mama's house.

This was my routine every single school day. My mother was consistent, dependable, and loving. She also meant business about the budget. Every day, she gave me $2.25 to include my $0.75 bus fare, $1.00 school lunch, and $0.50 for my after-school snack. I knew if I ever veered from the budget, I would just have to suck it up for the rest of the mealtimes that day and deal with the consequences.

One day, I had a bright idea. While waiting at Val's Liquor Store, I was staring at all the candy—candy I knew that I could not (or should not) purchase if I was to get through the day. I also knew that at my school, there were no vending machines or candy stores. The only options were to get breakfast or lunch in the cafeteria. Like most schools, Saint Anthony served rectangular-shaped pizza slices with a side of whole kernel corn on Fridays. I'm still a little baffled how pizza and corn went well-ish together… and apparently, it still makes an appearance on public school menus. Go figure.

That said, Friday had the best option offered for lunch. Pizza! And students whose parents had a little bit of money would get two (or maybe even three) slices of pizza on Fridays. Whereas, for me, this was not my reality.

But I had a plan.

One Monday morning, I decided to give it a shot. After going to Big Mama's house, sleeping for an hour, and walking to the bus stop, I arrived at Val's Liquor Store with a different thought in mind—and the courage to take a chance.

If you don't take a chance, you don't have a chance.

If you don't take a chance,
you don't have a chance.

While I was standing in Val's Liquor Store, I took the $2.25 and put $.75 in one pocket. With the remaining $1.50, I purchased three packs of Now and Laters for $.50 each. This was a very popular candy among kids, and each pack contained 12 individually wrapped pieces. I put the three packs of Now and Laters in my backpack. When the bus arrived, I paid my $.75 fare and was on my way to the marketplace—er, I mean *school*. My plan was to sell three individually wrapped pieces of candy for $.25 each. By doing so, I would double my investment.

Before school started, the students would gather in the cafeteria, where we would talk and play makeshift games like thump, paper-football field goal, or hand slap. Occasionally, there would be studying going on in the mornings, but most students usually did their homework at home. This was a prime opportunity to open up shop. The first day I started to offer candy at school, I made 12 sales by lunch. This meant I was completely out of inventory and holding $3.00 in exchange for that morning's $1.50. It worked!

Tuesday, it worked again.

Wednesday and Thursday as well.

Even the teachers would buy candy from me. It was wonderful!

And then there was Friday. When lunchtime rolled around, I felt like I could hear the classic football chant "We Ready" growing louder and louder in my ears. When I reached the pizza station in the lunch line, I asked for three pieces of pizza and gladly paid for them all. This was the beginning of a new routine, and I loved it. I was able to set and achieve the goal of having more pizza on Friday. I also avoided stressing out my mother. This was important to me because I felt that after the death of my father, the best thing I could do for her was to relieve some stress and not be a burden. I was also able to contribute and not put extra pressure on my mother for my childish desires.

This went on for a while until the one bad memory that I have from Saint Anthony occurred.

At the time, there was no policy against children selling candy at school. It wasn't even something people thought of at the time. That is, until one little girl told the nuns that I was buying candy and selling it to make a profit. Of course, the nuns insisted I stop.

At 9 years old, I hadn't researched how healthy school food was or wasn't, nor had I surveyed the diets of fourth-graders when they were away from school. I also knew that my three packs of Now and Laters were not going to shift the axis of the Earth or be any more harmful than the street in which I caught the bus. But, for the time being, I hung up my spurs and stopped selling candy.

I learned a lot from my time at St. Anthony, and my first lessons in business, but there were also some things I didn't learn. I didn't learn how to recognize a hater, and unfortunately, I would have to repeat that lesson again.

What I *did* learn was entrepreneurialism, risk-taking, helping the family, and doing things on my own—foundational components of adulthood that came naturally to me at an early age and would guide me for years to come.

(Lots of) Loss

ENTER MY NEXT BLESSING and big brother, Kenneth Gwyn. Considering what was about to happen, God knew I would need him. He and I met through Big Brothers and Sisters when I was about 9 years old. Big Brothers and Sisters is a nonprofit organization that pairs children with mentors to form a "big brother little brother" or "big sister and little sister" relationship.

Kenny took me by the hand and never let go. He's seen me cry, and he's seen me celebrate. He inserted himself into a really tough situation, and I can never thank him enough for that. Stepping into my life to be a brother was everything for me at such a critical time. Kenny lived near Kimball High School and had a swimming pool in his backyard. We rarely swam in it, but the oak trees in the neighborhood sure provided plenty of practice in learning pool maintenance. Over the years, Kenny taught me invaluable lessons like how to drive a stick shift car in the empty parking lot of the State Fair of Texas.

In 1984, Kenny was able to get tickets to the unattainable Victory Tour, featuring none other than Michael Jackson (and his brothers, of course). The King of Pop held concerts for three days at Texas Stadium, the home of the Dallas Cowboys. Kenny worked for the mayor at the time and pulled off a miracle. I quickly learned that having one real brother on your side can bring victory to anyone.

I got to know Kenny's family as well. His brother, Jimmy, was a decorated pilot, and his nephew, Keith, was a poster child for the Marines's esprit de corps. I admired and looked up to both, now gone to be with the Father. Keith was killed in action. Kenny's wife, Mary, is as regal as a queen and as revered as Clair Huxtable. Their son, Jake, is my little brother. It's a blessing to see the circle complete itself. Kenny poured into me, and now I get to pour into Jake. Everyone wins.

Losing Keith was rough on Kenny's family and me. Keith was the perfect Marine recon soldier, and I wanted to follow in his footsteps. Unfortunately, death was something I got used to. After the death of my father, I lost a lot of relatives on my mother's side of the family. We lost my Aunt Mary, Aunt Betty, Uncle Riley, Uncle Ben, Cousin Ben, Uncle Leo, Uncle Bobby, Aunt Ruby, and my grandmother (Big Mama)—all by the time I was in high school.

These people were not distant relatives; in fact, they all played huge roles in my life. Aunt Mary owned The

Black Inn restaurant, located next door to Val's. Uncle Ben was married to her and would let all the kids in the family play Pac-Man on his arcade machine. Aunt Betty lived next door to the YMCA, where I learned to swim. That was also where I volunteered with AT&T in 2016 to build a completely new playground and garden over what was previously an open field. Uncle Bobby used to play math games with me after school. Big Mama's house was Family Headquarters. Aunt Ruby introduced me to Top Ramen and every possible variation (cheese, sriracha, spaghetti sauce, and more) to stretch them further. Uncle Leo was very close to his brother Bobby, who lost a battle with laryngeal throat cancer. This weighed on Uncle Leo quite a bit, and he passed away the following year.

The day Uncle Leo died, I was at Big Mama's house, and she asked me to let him know that she had cooked dinner. I did as instructed; however, I discovered Uncle Leo in his room unresponsive. The paramedics came quickly, but he was already gone.

These were family members who were very close to me and, unfortunately, all left this world too soon. These experiences taught me to value the time we have with our loved ones. You never know when it could all end. Learn all you can while you can, and always be good to people close to you. Anything less is immature.

Learn all you can while you can,
and always be good
to people close to you.
Anything less is immature.

Just Trust Me

THE YEAR MY SISTER GRADUATED HIGH SCHOOL, so did Larry Johnson (a.k.a. Grand-MaMa, basketball phenom). The year before that, Michael Johnson, the Olympic Legend, graduated from Skyline High School. I started my freshman year after Larry and Angelia graduated. You can probably imagine what I was thinking at the time.

- ✓ Larry's from South Dallas, and so am I.
- ✓ He likes basketball, and so do I.
- ✓ He's like 6 feet 10 inches tall, and I'm like 5 feet 4 inches tall. Close enough.

I tried out for the basketball team, and it went exactly how I did *not* expect it to go. Coach Mayo (who coached Larry) put all the basketball hopefuls on different teams and had us switch positions, switch teams, and switch games three or four times during every day of tryouts. My teams won all of our games, but I was not selected to be on the basketball team.

Well, that was disappointing.

My mother then asked me if I would be interested in joining JROTC. Like I mentioned in the previous chapter, I initially said no, until she asked if I would join "for her." *Oh boy.* So, of course, I said yes and joined in the spring semester. What I quickly learned is that there were different parts of JROTC, including a group called the Rifle Drill Team. Well, I really liked that group. They had ceremonial rifles and conducted complex drill exercises that were amazing to watch (and be a part of). The rifles were M1903-A3 .30 caliber rifles that weighed over eight pounds.

Before you raise your eyebrows, the rifles had a rod of lead shoved down the barrel, making them inoperable. They are ceremonial, not weapons. Thankfully, I was able to demonstrate enough skill and made the team. While everyone else was a senior, I was the only freshman. It was harmonious. We were all committed to perfection, and it showed. In fact, for the first time, Skyline won the district championship that year.

And then it happened. All of the seniors graduated, which left me alone to rebuild the team and defend our championship. That summer, I found an iron pole in the garage that was about as long as a rifle and weighed about 10 pounds. I practiced every single team member's position in the front yard every day that summer until I knew them all by heart. The following year, I recruited some of my friends to join the team, and they recruited some of their friends. There were a few folks who were interested from the beginning, and with them, we had our team. Our first competition was out of town in Wichita Falls, Texas. We had a blast on the bus ride out there, but when it came time for the competition, we failed miserably.

After the competition, I gathered the team together privately.

I said, "If you trust me, and if you will follow me, I promise you we will never lose again." I explained that we had recently won the district championship, and I knew exactly what it took to win it again. They just had to trust me.

And that is exactly what happened. Going forward, we won every competition we entered. We were the first JROTC team ever to win the Dallas district championship three years in a row. During senior year, people started driving, working jobs, and juggling the responsibilities of taking care of things at home. Although we all loved JROTC and championships, there were competing priorities. I had to respect that. Although we didn't win the district championship our senior year, we did place fourth overall in state, and I won an individual state championship competition. I also won the Patrick Henry Medallion of Patriotism for exemplary leadership, performance, and spirit (with a broken toe). I'm not the person to give up when the going gets tough.

Leave the Wheel...

AT 17 YEARS OLD, when I was a senior in high school, I noticed that the brakes on the car I was driving were getting squeaky. It was a Chevy Cavalier with a five-speed manual transmission. I loved that car. When I told my mother about the squeaky brakes and we came to the conclusion I probably needed to replace them, she suggested that I speak with my Uncle Fatty, Aunt Dorothy's husband, to teach me how to change them. This was a lesson I knew I needed to learn, and it would turn out to be something that would carry me into adulthood.

I visited my Uncle Fatty and he immediately gave me instructions. The first thing he had me do was engage the emergency brake and "break the lugs." This meant loosening up each of the five lug nuts that held the tire onto the wheel, just enough to break the initial tension. Next, he instructed me to raise the car with the car jack. Now, the jack that I was using was the factory type that you must spin around in a circle as it slowly screws through the configuration and raises the vehicle. The jack was functional, but it was flimsy.

Of course, I didn't know that at the time.

Once I jacked the car up, he instructed me to completely remove the lug nuts from the screws that hold on the wheel. He shared that it's always important to put the lug nuts on the hubcap or off to the side so they don't get lost. Then, another important lesson. He told me to remove the wheel from the car and lay it on the ground, halfway underneath the car, just under the door. This was a crucial step because if the jack failed, the car would fall on the wheel. It would then be easier to raise the car back up because it would rest on the wheel instead of the ground.

Uncle Fatty walked me through the rest of the process, and we successfully completed the task. The brakes worked perfectly—they were silent and didn't shake. Life was good.

Fast forward a year or so down the road, and I noticed a small oil leak on the Cavalier. *No problem*. I had the seal/gasket around the oil pan replaced, and I thought I was good to go. However, I still noticed an oil leak that persisted. After doing some research, it seemed like the screws holding the oil pan to the car were not fully tightened after the gasket was replaced. So, I decided to fix this (seemingly small) issue myself.

A few days later, while parked at home in my mother's driveway, I began to take on the task of tightening up the screws holding my oil pan to stop the oil leak. Just as Uncle Fatty advised, I used my lug wrench to break the lugs and raise the car up using the spiral car jack. I removed the lugs from the wheels, set them to the side, and put the tire halfway under the car, just underneath the hinge of the front door.

At that point, I grabbed a 10-millimeter socket, a 6-inch socket extender, and a small quarter-inch socket wrench. I connected the three pieces and slid underneath the front of the vehicle until I could get to the oil pan and found the screws that I needed to tighten. Thankfully, there were only a couple. I tightened one screw and then started on the second screw. As I began to tighten it, I looked to the right and saw the jack starting to tilt.

Yikes.

Seeing that the car was about to fall at any moment, my heart rate doubled, and I started to sweat. I knew I didn't have very many options or much time. As I saw the car begin to fall, I turned my head to the side and got my 150-pound body as flat to the ground as I possibly could. Then it happened. *Boom!* The car fell.

By the grace of God, it landed on the wheel. The wheel might've been nine inches thick, and the transmission was just above my face. The oil pan and engine touched my chest as I wiggled out from the front of the car, oil stains all over my shirt, face, and back.

When I stood up, I had the heebie-jeebies. My sister was in the house with no idea what was happening outside. Good thing, too, because if my sister or mother would have found out, I would have been in serious trouble!

It was a while before I would crawl under a car again, and even then, only after I've really rocked it to make sure it's stable. For those unfamiliar with this type of mishap, people don't usually survive. Like, ever. It's a little heebie-jeebie for me right now just thinking about it! This was just one instance that I would later come to realize was evidence that God really did have a purpose for my life. No person, place, or thing would ever come in between His purpose and my life. As Big Mama would say, "Church ain't always on Sundays."

"Church ain't always on Sundays."

Ball till We Fall

A SHORT TIME after I graduated high school, I moved out of my mother's home and shared a 1,000-square-foot apartment with one of my best friends, Trayl. It was a great apartment, and we never had any issues with any neighbors. Everyone was very respectful, and we were excited to finally be on our own. On the weekends, we often played basketball. One day, a group of us agreed to play basketball in a nearby suburb called Garland, Texas.

That day, a number of us decided to play ball, including Trayl, my cousin Harold, Damien, Alonzo, D. Berry, and a few other friends. Damien and Harold were (and still are) best friends. At the time, Damien, also known as Dee, attended college at Texas A&M Commerce and proudly played defensive end on their football team. He was home for summer break, so we played a lot of ball.

"Two hundred and forty pounds of twisted steel," he would say as he owned the paint like Shaquille O'Neal.

If Dee was on your side, you loved it. If not, well… not so much. On this particular day, the basketball courts seemed to have one hoop that was a little lower than the 10-foot regulation height. So, after a couple of full-court games, we switched to half-court on the lower goal. This was, inevitably, a dunk-fest. Granted, everyone could dunk on a regulation goal, but at 9 feet, 8 inches tall, you could have some real fun. We must have played "every player for themselves" for half an hour.

Now, Dee and I are very close friends, but at the time, we had a slight rivalry. Since Harold and I are first cousins, we were always close like brothers. We are one year apart, went to almost all the same schools together, and often spent the night at each other's homes. Dee lived in the same neighborhood as Harold, so they also hung out a lot and grew up together. I used to spend the night at Harold's after all the neighborhood kids had to go home. Dee would have to leave, so Harold and I would keep the (kid) party going. This was especially important on the weekend when we would watch Michael Jordan's *Come Fly with Me* VHS tape over and over.

So, it was common for Dee and me to bicker a little bit. Nothing major, just a little debate every once in a while. Here's where I would say, "If you know Dee, then you know what I mean." He would say the same about me, and we both would laugh. Then both of us would silently mouth, "It's really him."

Alright. Back to the game.

Coincidentally, every time I went up to dunk, Dee was there to stop me. To put this into perspective, Dee was 6 feet 3 inches tall with 240 pounds of muscle, while I was 6 feet 3 inches tall, and 160 pounds soaking wet. And after years of believing I could be "like Mike," that day, I went toe-to-toe with Dee every time I got the ball. As you can imagine, I was exhausted after the game. As everyone went their separate ways, Trayl and I went home. I can't remember what Trayl did afterward, but I went straight to bed and laid down while it was still mid-afternoon.

When I woke up a few hours later, I had a hard time wrapping my mind around what was happening. There is this thing they call "the devil riding your back" (a.k.a. sleep paralysis). When you wake up and your eyes are still closed, but you're conscious and mentally trying to tell your eyes to open, that brief amount of time is the paralysis. This usually lasts a few seconds, but rarely ever more than a full minute. However, this experience of mine lasted way more than a minute, and it wasn't something that I could mentally make go away.

When I woke up, it was maybe eight in the evening. I could see around my room, knew where I was, and knew who I was. I also knew that I had been playing basketball earlier. But when I tried to get out of the bed, I couldn't. My legs would not respond. *Strange*. I was trying not to panic. My mind was starting to move faster, and I started asking myself questions.

What is really going on?

I started troubleshooting the situation. I could see that I could move my arms, head, and neck, but I couldn't move my legs. I used my hands to touch my thighs and felt my fingers on my legs, so I knew I still had feeling in my lower extremities. I quickly got resourceful and grabbed my bed's headboard. Using it for leverage, I pulled myself up and somewhat twisted my body so that my legs were hanging off the bed. Thankfully I was able to position myself in a sitting-upright position.

I could then further diagnose myself and see that I could wiggle my toes. So, I could move my feet a little, but I couldn't walk. In fact, I thought that if I tried to stand, I might fall. My roommate wasn't home, so I was on my own. However, things really heated up when I started to realize I needed to make my way to the restroom to relieve myself, and the struggle escalated with an unstoppable bodily function meeting a pair of immovable legs. After my to-and-from commute to the restroom in the crawl lane, I was thinking I had to fix this. I knew I was going to need some help.

Trayl was away, so I called Harold on the phone and told him what was happening. He was worried, wondering if he might need to take me to the hospital. When he offered to take me, I didn't take him up on it. I think I was in denial, refusing to believe this was going to be my permanent future. However, I knew I needed someone to help me, so I called Alonzo, one of the guys who played ball with us earlier that day. Alonzo came to my aid with no hesitation. He came over to my apartment immediately and stayed until I went to the doctor the next day. When it was time to visit the doctor, he really did the most he could do to help me. To get in or out of a car, I would unbuckle my seatbelt, Alonzo leaned in while I hugged him, and then he'd stand me up out of the vehicle. Even though I could move my arms and crutch, I couldn't put weight on my legs, so he'd hand me one crutch and physically be my other crutch. I refused to use the wheelchair. This became our normal routine when a doctor's visit was needed.

During this time, I went to a doctor's office that was nearby. A woman owned the practice, and she did her absolute best to help me get well. After many, many X-rays, she was finally able to see that I was suffering from a hairline fracture just below the last vertebrae (L5) of my spine, the sacrum. Since that bone was still intact, she believed that even though it was fractured, it would set properly and heal if I got plenty of rest and didn't move much. For nearly four weeks, Alonzo stayed at my side. He helped me move around my apartment, went to the store to get groceries and essentials when I couldn't, and was my support during the ever-uncomfortable doctor's visits. And after four (long) weeks, the doctor was absolutely right. I regained mobility in my legs, the pain subsided, and I was on a pathway to recovery.

Now, I was the kind of kid who didn't like to bring drama to my mother. So, if I had an issue or got into a bind, she was the absolute last person I would call. Not that I couldn't call her, but I felt that after all that she went through with my father's suicide, raising my sister and me, and the many hardships we had been through, the least I could do was not cause her any additional stress. Even now, I ask for very little and take responsibility for my actions.

A couple of years later, Harold, Dee, Alonzo, and I won our division in a three-on-three basketball tournament called Hoop It Up. Our team name was *Ball till We Fall*. It was one of the most physically exerting contests I've ever participated in, and I was elated that Dee was on our team. But coming back from the back injury, I was even more overjoyed that I had a fully functioning body again.

There were so many teachable moments during that time, but most importantly, I learned that health is the greatest wealth. There are five wealths: wealth of the mind, wealth of the house/family, financial wealth, health wealth, and spiritual wealth. To gain the understanding and importance of health at 19 years old was priceless. I also learned the importance of being good to people who are good to you. And lastly, it's good to slow down... sometimes.

Health is the greatest wealth.

OK, I didn't learn to slow down at 19 years old, but I do believe God was giving me some downtime. Hallelujah.

Flight 592

I WAS ONCE ON A PLANE that crashed. True story.

There used to be this airline company called ValuJet. It was, as the name implies, a low-cost airline, and the central hub was in Atlanta, Georgia. No matter where you flew in the country, if you flew ValuJet, you were going to have a connecting flight through Atlanta. On May 11, 1995, I was in North Carolina visiting friends and making a return to Dallas, Texas. I was flying ValuJet; therefore, my connection was from Raleigh/Durham to Atlanta. Thankfully, the layover wasn't bad. It was the last flight of the night, and everyone was anxious to get home.

When I landed in Atlanta, my connecting flight to Dallas was boarding shortly thereafter in the same terminal, not far from the gate at which I landed. As usual, everyone boarded the plane and sat patiently (or not so patiently) waiting to take off, and the flight crew went through the typical pre-flight safety checks and explanations. What was unique about ValuJet is that the flight attendants always had a lot of fun. Although they were doing the safety check, they sang through the handout like a song from a musical, complete with hand motions. People actually paid attention to the safety briefings, which was very cool. However, what was *not* cool was sitting at the gate.

After about 45 minutes of sitting at the gate, the pilot came on the speaker, "Good evening, ValuJet passengers! We are experiencing some trouble with maintenance issues, and we're working to get them resolved as soon as we can. Please be patient with us." The groaning and grumbling from the passengers floated through the cabin. But at least there was some sort of end in sight.

Not too much later, his voice came back on. "We're still having issues, but we are bringing another plane to the gate next to ours. Hang tight, and we'll have you file off this plane and board the other. Your luggage will be moved over, and we'll get you on your way shortly!"

Way to go, ValuJet. I mean, it kinda felt like concierge service.

We were all happy that we would be pushing off soon, so we all gladly deboarded the first plane and boarded the second, saying our goodbyes to the first crew, who did their best to entertain us while we were sitting there. Just as the original pilot advised, the second plane was ready to go as soon as we boarded. It was an uneventful flight, and we landed safely in Dallas.

That's when the craziness started.

As soon as I turned my cellphone back on, I began to receive phone calls from friends and family members. It was a little strange because, although everyone enjoys a warm welcome home, this seemed urgent... and dire. It wasn't long before I found out that the news reported that Flight 592 had recently crashed in the Everglades in an attempt to fly to Miami. I suppose they thought the plane was fixed and tried to conduct one more flight that night.

A total of 108 people perished on that plane. If any of the souls survived the crash, the alligator habitat would have been impossible to overcome. It was surreal to think about. I can still remember some of the conversations on the plane and the fun atmosphere that crew was trying to create. My heart went out to all the families of the people on Flight 592.

Much like the day the car fell over me, I can look back on that day and know God saved me and had a special purpose for my life. It was one of those "footprints in the sand" moments where we look back and see one set of footprints and realize it was then that God carried us.

Anomalies are born into these all-or-nothing experiences, where one thing can change the course of our lives. Experiences where there is nothing to hold onto but faith. For most of us, somewhere along the journey into our adult lives, we start listening to logic and reason and shun child-like faith away. That's the evil trick life pulls on so many people. The key is to counter logic and reason with vision and belief.

I'll leave it at this for now: Nothing can stop us... but us. *Nothing.* So, don't ever stop or give up.

Nothing can stop us but us, and nothing is over until God says it's over.

ChelloooOOOooo

I ONCE MET PRINCE. I really didn't realize how big of a deal this was until I later told a good friend of mine, Angellah Zenith, about the story. She just about passed out.

But let's rewind.

I'm fortunate enough to be good friends with the Badu family, as in Erykah Badu. She is the multi-platinum recording artist turned legend after she ushered in an entirely new genre of music, Baduizm/Neo-soul.

Dallas is a big city, but often I've found that there are very few degrees of separation between many of us. Erykah's younger brother knows friends of mine from the neighborhood. I also became great friends with her sister, Koryan, also known as Koko, when I began to do freelance sound engineering at SCQ Studios. The owner of SCQ Studios, Craig Sweet, would soon become an amazing mentor to me. Craig had a 7,000 square-foot two-story facility where we later filmed movies, held events, and leveraged for photoshoots. You could meet almost anyone from the "who's who" of Dallas at Craig's studio. Often, on-air personalities from the largest radio stations would be there. Not coincidentally, the facility was just around the corner from one of those radio stations, K104. There were also producers, singers, musicians, and all sorts of talent that would be working at SCQ Studios.

There are dozens of stories of us leaving SCQ, going over to some friend's home, and keeping the party going until we went back to SCQ the following day. Many days, 360 (one of Craig's producers) and I would work around the clock in the studio, never going further than the Jack in the Box restaurant across the street. We would work until we couldn't, sleep under the studio stage lights for warmth, and then go right back to the music. The bottom line is that I really honed my sound engineering skills at this studio and worked with national talent like Tony Terry and Rasheedah, and lots of artists from Texas.

Today, Erykah Badu's birthday parties are huge and still a little hard to get into. But back in the day, they were *very* private. Invitation only. As I mentioned earlier, her sister, Koryan, and I are great friends. We all live our own lives, so we're not always in each other's space. However, every so often, Koko invited a couple friends and me to Erykah's birthday party.

I'll never forget the first time she invited me.

Erykah owned the Forest Theater in South Dallas off Highway 175 and Martin Luther King, Jr. Boulevard. It has an incredibly tall green and red structure that stands high above the roof of the building, and it's about as iconic in South Dallas as the State Fair of Texas. The Forest Theater is a truly iconic building, and it was owned by a Black woman from South Dallas with green eyes. (Stop trying to put people in boxes, y'all.)

Everyone in Dallas knows Erykah is a little over the top. Everything Erykah does is surprising, entertaining, or both. You just know she's going to always bring the "wow" factor in everything she does.

When I arrived at the Forest Theater the day of her birthday party, I was met at the door by the Fruit of Islam. You know, the guys with the bowties who are in positions of security. They checked my invitation and allowed me to proceed through the door. Once inside, I noticed a bottle of Courvoisier liquor and champagne on *every* table. Shortly after, I connected with a few familiar faces. A Dallas promoter, a couple of music producers, and I gathered around and started to talk. The place was dripping with celebrities like Big Gipp and his wife, Joi. Gipp, Ceelo Green, and a couple others make up the group Goodie Mob. Roy Ayers (who's made music with Whitney Houston and Jill Scott) was in the building, as well as Bilal (who has collabs with Beyoncé and Kendrick Lamar) and Musiq Soulchild (multi-platinum R&B artist). Common was also there and in rare form.

As I took everything in, a lady walked up to my circle of friends. She was super nice. Like strawberry shortcake on a random Wednesday nice.

"Hey now, how y'all doing? Y'all having a good time?" she cooed.

It was Chaka Khan. She looked like an angel with gorgeous, long-flowing hair. Her skin radiated, even in the dimly lit facility, and her smile brightened up the whole room. Some people are just born impressive. She is one of them.

As the night went on, the list continued to grow. We managed to keep it cool until suddenly, one guy turned to me and said, "Damn, you know you got to be doing it if Prince shows up at your birthday party."

My eyes widened as I thought, *Prince? Prince like Purple Rain vs. Thriller, Prince?!*

I looked over my shoulder. Sure enough, His Royal Badness, The Artist, The Purple Rain Piano Picasso was standing not three feet from me. Yep, you're definitely doing it right when Prince shows up at your birthday party. As I stood there, I reasoned that there was no way on God's green Earth that Prince was going to show up in South Dallas on Martin Luther King Boulevard and not have a conversation with me.

You're definitely doing it right
when Prince shows up
at your birthday party.

Now, let's keep some things in perspective. Everyone was talking to everyone. It was chill. Remember, Erykah is the Queen of Neo-soul, and everyone had a very relaxed vibe the entire evening. However, Prince was the only person in the entire building who had security with him. He had three bodyguards who were larger than any other humans I'd seen in my life. I mean, I didn't know they made humans that big!

I was starting to question whether those three men would be interested in playing for the Dallas Cowboys so we could go back and win a few more Super Bowls.

I digress. Back to the party.

I could hear Prince having a conversation, but I wasn't dialed in to exactly what was being said. Then, the magical moment arrived: I heard the conversation end. I knew this was the opportunity for me. Now, at that point in my life, I hadn't put on a lot of weight. I was still a pretty thin guy and could fit into places not many could, so before anyone else struck up a conversation with the Minnesota miracle, I made my move.

I leaned right in between two of the largest people I'd ever seen in my life, looked at Prince, and said the first thing that came to mind. With a quick yet cool nod of my head, I casually said to Mr. Red Corvette, "Wassup?"

Cringe.

Prince then did something that I don't think I've ever seen another man do. He looked me dead in the eyes, coming off a bit like he was surprised that I had spoken to him. But I knew he was actually checking to try to figure out who the hell I was. He must have looked me up and down about eight or nine times, then met my eyes again. Just before he turned his head away from me to direct his attention back toward someone approaching him, he said, "ChelloooOOOooo."

I turned back to the guys who were watching the whole interaction play out, and they looked a little bewildered. "Hey, man. What just happened?" one of them asked.

And so, I tried to summarize and interpret what just happened by saying, "It's cool. He's from Minnesota. That's how they say hello."

There was another unique Prince moment that happened that night, but I'll save that one for the next book. So, that evening I met Prince—the 26-instrument playing "Purple Rain"-making legend—in the flesh! Wow! I went into that night knowing that Koryan and Erykah cared enough to expose a young guy from their ZIP code to a really fly lifestyle. And I'm forever grateful for their kindness and realness. I'm blessed to say that wasn't the only time we had some amazing moments together, but it was definitely one that a few of us still giggle about from time to time.

That night, I learned that the absolute best of the best men *and* women are within reach. Just go for it! And always be cool.

The absolute best of the best
men *and* women are within reach.
Just go for it!

Stay Changed

MY FIRST ROLE WITH SBC (now AT&T) was a non-management role. I wanted to work as an outside technician, and since I didn't know much about the work, I went to the Dallas Public Library and picked up a few books. I was able to put together enough content, memorize it, and pass the technical test the following day. In fact, during the onboarding process, I took the tests for both an outside technician role and a customer service role, and I passed both. However, at the time, I was only offered the call center role. The outside technician role paid more, had more autonomy, and focused on working with my hands—something I was really good at. The customer service role was specific to central office operations, where I would work in an office building and communicate with technicians who worked in centralized (telephone) offices with computers and machines that create features like dial tone and call waiting.

After I accepted the customer service role, they told me that if I had declined the first offer, they would've offered me a technician role. Yeah, I agree it was a different world back then, but what I didn't know at the time is that God was about to park an angel just an arm's reach from me.

The central office role carried the title of customer service representative, and it was pretty interesting. We managed a huge worklist, performed testing on different circuits or phone lines, and assigned central office technicians if we were unable to resolve the matter. We had capabilities like metallic loop testing, loopback testing, and more. We worked in a UNIX-based system.

After being trained and learning how to perform my job manually, I began to poke around in the system and found where I could build macros. A macro is a single instruction that will automatically perform a series of instructions to complete a particular task. While working in this role, I figured out a way to create multiple macros that would do all sorts of things. The first set of macros I created was able to grab a ticket off the work list and assign it to myself. The next set of macros I created would complete the top four or five subsequent actions. Finally, the last set of macros would close the tickets out. I used these macros myself, and I was able to complete five or six times as much work as my peers. Eventually, I loaded the macros on everyone's computer... in the entire department.

We went from having an average of 40 pages of tickets to never having more than one page. Additionally, any tickets that arrived on the work list were picked up within seconds. This process was one of the first automations I created. I started small and learned what it took to get a "change" to stay "changed." It felt great to implement a new process that would make our department 10 times faster, and I knew I wasn't done.

Training Simulation

DURING MY TIME IN THAT FIRST ROLE as a non-management employee, I had a few different managers. Shirley Baker was my first manager, and I loved her.

She once told me, "Never introduce yourself as just David. Always say David Williams. You're smart, and people are going to need to know who you are."

Then there was José, a really smart guy who didn't stay long as my manager. He went on to do well for himself. The following manager I had was the first Black man I ever worked for, whom I won't name here. Since he was new, I tried to show him the work that the department did, but he really wasn't that interested and didn't take the time to learn. However, what I learned from him is something I'll never forget. He often engaged in informal discussions with me, and then those discussions would show up as written discussions in my personnel file.

I had the least amount of seniority, so my schedule was horrible. Some weeks I would work the dayshift, then the next week, I would work evenings, and then overnight shifts the week after. I never had two off days together; they were always split. For low-seniority employees, bad schedules were common in the workplace.

So, one week, my schedule required that I work overnight shifts. During the overnight shift, there were only about six folks who worked at one time. We worked in a building just off the south side of Interstate I-30 called Pinnacle Park. It was the first building in the area, and there was literally nothing else around. Thankfully, at least the road on which the building was located had been recently extended and paved. It was common to see different wildlife in the parking lot at night: rabbits, turtles, coyotes, and all sorts of things.

When you worked an overnight shift, 15-minute breaks and lunches were often used for naps. It was very common to see employees log out for a break or lunch, find a vacant desk, set an alarm, and lay their heads down to get some shut-eye.

Well, my manager wrote me up for one such nap and enforced a DML (Decision-Making Leave). Many would refer to a DML as "one foot in the grave and the other on a banana peel." If you made any mistake in performance or attendance after a DML, you would be fired on the spot. The DML lasted for 12 months. So, for the next 12 months, I had to be perfect in attendance and performance.

However, for the first time, I filed a grievance. A grievance is a formal complaint, usually to counter/overturn a previous decision. I filed a grievance during this DML period, in which the grievance took 19 months to resolve. And what was the resolution, you might ask? Well, I won the case, and all the inaccuracies and non-facts were removed.

I learned some valuable lessons through this whole ordeal: Not everyone who acts like they support you actually does support you. All skin folk ain't kinfolk. No matter how good you are in your craft or how good you are to people, there will always be someone who doesn't like you. Sometimes, they may even have a higher title. And, most importantly, I learned that what God has for you, no one can take from you.

What God has for you,
no one can take from you.

I lost my dad at a very early age. I hoped that there would be a Black male leader who would work with me to help me reach my potential. I really wanted to bond with a leader, work to do great things together, and have someone I could learn from. That hadn't occurred yet.

But now, enter God's timing.

After the grievance, I stayed in that role for another year and a half. During this time, I met some amazing people.

My previous supervisor later got into another situation with another employee who had 25 years with the company. She knew the grievance process much better than I did, and he was later demoted to non-management and moved to a different department.

My next supervisor was a woman named Dee Watson. She was a Black woman and an absolute angel in my eyes. Dee was kind to me and gave me incredible opportunities. While on her team, I worked on a project that focused on improving how fast our largest circuits (DS3 and optical) were installed. We were able to close some gaps that mitigated potential government-agency penalties. I led the project across five states and we drove a $10-million return on investment (ROI).

During this time, I also met one of the most influential folks in my life, Linda Denise Jackson. AT&T had dozens of employee groups for all ethnicities and interests, and Linda was the president of the Dallas/Fort Worth Employee Resource Group, Community NETwork (later changed to The NETwork), which was an affinity group for Black people. Linda worked her magic and filed the aforementioned grievance. She fought tooth and nail, day and night until it was completely resolved. And once it was behind us, we were on a mission.

Linda introduced me to the concept of mentoring through ERGs. Prior to that time, Kenny and a few uncles were the only folks who personally invested their time and resources to share wisdom and insight with me so that I would have a better future. Linda came through in a big way. She asked me to join her mentoring circle committee. While in this role, I attended several mentoring circles each month, as well as meeting with officers to request their participation in the mentoring program. I used a ton of my vacation time to attend all those meetings, but it was well worth it. I've since encouraged many to participate in mentoring.

Linda would often say, "To get something you never had before, you must be willing to do something you've never done before." Linda introduced me to greats like Earl Graves Sr., the founder of Black Enterprise magazine, and Ray Wilkins, a Black man who was a Level two manager for 11 years. He ended his 32-year career as CEO of AT&T Innovation & Yellow Pages working directly for the chairman.

Linda also introduced me to many high-ranking officers and taught me about Granville T. Woods and other Black inventors. She was a gift.

About a year after meeting Linda, I left that department, but I would never leave her.

From there, I transitioned over to the Consumer Broadband organization. The role was Tier 2 tech support, and the bulk of it was spent troubleshooting internet issues for residential customers and some small businesses. The internet was paired with some Yahoo services like email, online protection, and a few other features. The job was technical and cool, and I didn't have many issues with it... that is, until I started to aspire for more.

I guess this is a good time to mention something about my previous manager. Yes, the one who wrote me up on all that nonsense. The one who I grieved and won the grievance against. The one who was demoted to a call-taking representative role was now taking calls in this Tier 2 organization. Quite ironic, but wait, it gets better. There was another Black man who was a manager in this group who was not very fond of me, and he wouldn't entertain opportunities for me to advance my career. But after six months or so, he transferred to a different organization.

I then began to work with Myra Campbell and John Buquoi. They were both very kind to me. Myra was a Black woman, and John was an older white man. Myra was newer to the organization, and since I knew the work very well, I helped her with a few different things. John, on the other hand, had been around since the very beginning of the department and built the training program. I tried to learn all I could from John.

I became extremely proficient in my role. Within two or three minutes of talking to anyone, I could identify the problem and needed solution. However, I still couldn't find an opportunity for advancement. So, I changed my approach. Over time, I emulated John. John wore cargo pants, I wore cargo pants. John wore plaid shirts, I wore plaid shirts. I was trying to assimilate and figure out a way to get a chance to be seen. I thought that maybe if I looked more like him, then folks wouldn't be so afraid to give someone who looked different a shot, especially at a promotion. If the work I was producing wasn't good enough, I wanted to find out what could be good enough. Well, it was either the cargo pants or the past two years of great work, but my chance finally came in.

Our organization was looking to add or promote an additional trainer to the training team, and the first step was to hold a mock training class. There were three people competing for the role: myself, an older white man who had previously been a trainer, and a young white lady. Although I had phenomenal results and numbers, I was told I was not the favorite at the time. The training team had historically been very homogenous. They had recently added a woman of color to the team, so some dynamics were changing, but nothing was guaranteed.

For the mock training class, they assigned us each one topic and gave us one week to prepare. I did my best to perfect some PowerPoint slides, but PowerPoint was not my strong suit. It just wasn't coming together like it needed to. So, a couple days in, I stopped and looked at what I was doing and had to regroup. I thought to myself, *OK, the management team invited you to participate in this exercise, so there has to be something good that you're bringing to the table. Let's focus on that.*

I stepped back and looked at the topic I was tasked to deliver—Yahoo Online Protection. Most of the agents weren't too fond of this product, not because it was a bad product, but rather because you had to know the product by memory. There was nothing to guide you as you walked a customer through resetting it or configuring it for their specific needs. In fact, there were simulators for everything except this. Well, I had no access to software to create simulators, especially behind the AT&T firewall.

So, I used what I did have access to—Microsoft Excel. I opened a blank spreadsheet, removed the grid lines from the page, and captured 700 screenshots of the Yahoo Online Protection software. I then imported them all into my spreadsheet and placed hyperlinks over the buttons of the Yahoo Online Protection that would redirect to other cells in the worksheet. Therefore, by carefully placing the screenshots, I could have the hyperlinks point to other locations all around the worksheet and it would look like you were navigating through the application instead of jumping around the worksheet of Microsoft Excel.

And just like that, I had a working simulator.

During my section of training, most of the discussion would be around the simulator and how to use it, so I built a few PowerPoint slides to discuss the simulator. The audience I was delivering the content to would also be able to take something tangible with them that would reinforce the training itself—I loaded the simulators onto their computers. On the day of delivery, all three of us had to present our portion of training. I heard that the former trainer did pretty well. He was seasoned, he knew no strangers, and he was known for being a nice guy. However, the young lady who presented had some challenges. Public speaking is not easy. When it was time for me to present my material... I killed it. The entire hour could not have gone better, and the outcome was on par. I was named the newest trainer to the training team. I was so excited. I was actually making a tangible move in my career, and all the hard work, all the politics, all the emulating worked. It finally worked.

Creating that simulator was not easy. I spent dozens of hours building that solution. It was incredibly complex with all those screenshots and hyperlinks. It was also a super low-cost solution that yielded high benefits. This was a "making ends meet" and "a dollar out of 15 cents" transferable skill type of mentality showing up at the workplace. Like the car-jack-falling scenario, I had to figure out what to do in the moment. Or like when Angelia grabbed my hand that day in August, the decision on a new direction and taking next steps started immediately.

I had never built a simulator before, but ingenuity and innovation are born from necessity. I had been in tough situations before and although I didn't know to build a simulator, I did know that I needed to not give into my fears, but rather act on my faith. My passion for progress combined with years and years of troubleshooting problems led me to creating and building something that had not been done before. It also led me to discovering an internal confidence that I could do that new thing, too.

Peanut Butter and Jelly

AFTER LANDING THAT TRAINER JOB, I then loaded the simulator I created on the computers of 300 agents—about half in California and half in Texas. The agents loved it. I was glad I didn't give up when things were not so promising. I continued to deliver with high performance, waited for my opportunity, and seized it. Sometimes you just need God to move the wrong people out of your right-of-way, and success is sure to follow.

> Sometimes you just need God
> to move the wrong people out
> of your right-of-way,
> and success is sure to follow.

Because I did so well with the Yahoo Online Protection project, I was asked to participate in more project-related work, and I fell in love with project management. I had also begun to research project management certifications, beginning with one called the Project Management Professional (PMP). The company offered to pay for the course if you were already in a project management role… however, I was *not*. So, I saved up as much as I could and bought as much PMP content as possible. It was about $700 for the PMBOK book and digital study guide I needed. On a non-management salary, that's a lot of money.

About a year or so later, I began canvassing for management/promotion job opportunities. I had gone through about three interviews. All of them were over the phone, and none of them were dazzling or successful. So, I made a commitment to myself. I made up my mind that I was going to be unequivocally prepared for the next job interview. Short of Jesus Christ himself applying for the job, no one was going to beat me.

Sure enough, a job I had applied for a couple months prior reached out. The opportunity was for a role in the Dallas Internet Data Center. I gladly accepted the interview, confirmed it would be in-person, and immediately began my research. For those who don't know, data centers are where the internet lives. If you've ever wondered why Google never goes down (or any other website for that matter), it's because all that infrastructure lives in data centers. Data centers have multiple forms of electrical power that come into the building from different directions. They also have thousands of batteries and multiple generators in case the power goes down. They also have multiple forms of connectivity to keep the internet up and running. Data centers are usually hard to find and extremely secure, with a number of concrete barriers and trenches built into their architecture. Even in a large company the size of AT&T, there were only 20 of those specific PM jobs in the United States.

Before the interview, I drove to the location so I knew exactly where I could find the building and the door I needed to enter. I even wanted to know what security would be like on the day of the interview. I researched as much as I could online and picked up any and all internal training courses that were available. I also refreshed myself with the PMBOK book, so I could be as sharp as I could on any project-management-related questions.

Finally, the day of the interview arrived, and I met with two men named Mark and Burley. Mark was the supervisor, and Burley was the incumbent project manager on his way out. Burley already had a new job and was trying to help Mark find a replacement.

We got right to it, and Burley started asking me very technical questions like:

"What's the distance limitation of CAT5 Ethernet?"

"What is a network spanning tree?"

"What is the difference between single-mode and multi-mode fiber?"

Mark's questions, on the other hand, were very different. He started off saying, "Tell me three reasons a manhole is round."

When Mark asked this obscure question, I felt like it was a license for me to show my full personality. I thought, *Oh, OK. You want to see if I can think on my feet. You want to go there. You want to see creativity.*

Confident of my answer, I responded right away. "Three reasons a manhole is round. It's a circle, and because it's a circle, it'll never fall inside the manhole. Since it's heavy, it's easier to roll away than dragging or carrying it away if it was a rectangle or square. And that's it. I don't have a third answer."

Mark said, "We'll come back to that one. It's OK. Tell me this: If you could be a superhero, who would you be and why?"

At that point, I felt like he was testing me. And I was ready for the test. The question made me think back to an episode of a cartoon I watched as a child called "The Justice League". I remembered one episode where the Justice League did not want to allow Batman to be a member of their elite team because he didn't have any superhuman powers. Later in that cartoon episode, the Justice League faced a monster that was zapping superhero powers from the superheroes. Obviously, this did not impact Batman, who had his utility belt and amazing fighting skills. Batman saved the Justice League that episode, and, therefore, they allowed him to be a member. (Doesn't this sound a lot like "Rudolph the Red-Nosed Reindeer"?)

My mind was processing all of this in real-time. So, when Mark asked me the superhero question, I quickly replied, "I would be Batman."

"Why?"

"Batman doesn't have any superhuman powers, but I believe if you have the will, you can always develop the skill."

If you have the will,
you can always develop the skill.

Mark was a very matter-of-fact kind of manager and not easily swayed. But in that interview, after that response, I could see that he was impressed. However, that was only the beginning. I knew how much I had prepared for that day and moment. I knew what I brought to bear and what I had to offer. So, when he asked that last question and wanted me to "describe how I would project manage building a peanut butter and jelly sandwich," it was like God had pitched me a softball in a baseball game with the bases loaded.

Keep in mind, I had just purchased an expensive book that taught the entire project management theory. For this question, I felt like I was so ahead of my time, my parents hadn't even met me yet.

"First, I would discuss this initiative with the sponsor of the peanut butter and jelly sandwich project to ensure

I had authority to garner resources and understood the exact requirements. Then, there are several things that we would need to confirm in the initiating and planning phase before we begin the execution and monitoring phase of the project. Initially, we need to understand what time the peanut butter and jelly sandwich needs to be delivered— is it by lunch tomorrow? Lunch today? Before school, so you can take it with you? Does this peanut butter and jelly sandwich need to be toasted? Is it on white bread, wheat bread, or another specialty bread? Does the sandwich need to be cut? Does it need to have the edges around it?

"What type of peanut butter are we talking about? Is it creamy? Is it chunky? What type of jelly are we talking? Grape jelly? Strawberry jelly? How many sandwiches? Individually wrapped? Paper or plastic? Afterward, we would have some discussions to understand the lessons learned. This will ensure that we can perfect the process and make sure that we reduce any friction so that the next time we build a peanut butter and jelly sandwich, it's an even better experience. Lastly, we'll need to document and track results as we close the project out."

It was amazing! I crushed that interview.

Long after I left his organization, Mark and I shared a beer and a good laugh about that interview. It'll go down in the history books, I'm sure.

Serendipity
and Sweat Equity

I STARTED THE DATA CENTER JOB on September 16, 2008, which was a very unique time in American history. For the first time ever, there was a serious possibility that a Black man could become the President of the United States of America. I imagine many Black women feel the same way with electing our first Black woman to the White House. It was also the day the Great Recession started with the collapse of Lehman Brothers. For those in the investment community, you probably already know what this means. For those unfamiliar with this industry, it's simple. When the economy turns down, business revenues dry up, and investments follow suit. Small companies fail. Large companies right-size, which, at the time, meant many companies either exited data centers around the world or reduced the size of their footprint (amount of space their equipment needed) in the data center.

Our data center was huge, and we had just gone through an expansion. It had 168,000 square feet of sellable space (footprint), six huge generators, hundreds of UPS batteries, thousands of smoke detectors, hundreds of cameras, and a couple of hand scans to get in the building. Unfortunately, we lost a lot of customers when the recession hit—especially for a data center of our size.

Now, Mark, who was the second line manager, is sharp. No one knew the data center world like he did. In the very beginning, he told me that the job would change me. He told me it changed him, and there was nothing that he could do about it. I'm grateful that he was honest and transparent when he told me to buckle up. He was correct, as in the job would change me for the better. The job and Mark both trained me to never assume.

This was my first management role, and I was so thankful to God for the job that every day I wore a suit to work. Wearing a suit and tie to the data center was like a mechanic wearing a suit and tie to work. You're definitely a little overdressed, and you really better know what you're doing if you want to be respected. So, I focused on the work. And there was plenty of it.

Every day, I would use Ohm's Law to perform power calculations. Then I would use Ohm's Law to calculate how much cooling was needed to cool the equipment that we were powering. Even though I loved that job, it could be stressful. Mark told me, "If there's ever a fire, we get everybody out of the building. Then we run to the fire. Seriously."

One day, there was a fire alarm. Of course, this happened on a day when Mark wasn't in the building. So, there I was, reading the fire panel and flipping through blueprints to identify which of the 4,000 smoke detectors was giving an alarm. I guess it's worth mentioning that if you didn't get the smoke detector identified quickly, the fire alarm panel would automatically dispatch the fire department. They would show up in full gear and with axes. *Yikes.*

The data center was full of similar moments that would test and prove who you really were, and I always welcomed the challenge.

Data centers are a very cost-intensive business. The equipment, cabling, and everything in between must last a lifetime. For example, a power strip must last a lifetime. The strands of fiber and the connection tips of those strands of fiber must last a lifetime. The electrical work must last a lifetime. And for those services, the companies that provided and specialized in those specifics charged a premium compared to typical home and consumer goods. That said, I figured out a way to repurpose existing unused infrastructure instead of procuring new materials. I could get the work done faster and cheaper (or faster and free instead of spending funding that I was approved to spend). Over the next year or so, we closed several millions of dollars of projects with an accelerated ROI by repurposing and certifying!

When I first was hired by Mark, just a couple days into the job, I attended a really important meeting related to expanding the data center. All sorts of folks were there, including architects, designers, and financial stakeholders. Unfortunately, I noticed one person in attendance seemed to be a bit more interested in their own success than the overall success of the objective. I mentioned this to Mark privately after the meeting, and he agreed and thanked me for using discretion and not calling the person out in the meeting.

At the end of our conversation, he added, "Good job, Mr. Williams. I need you to bring everything to the table. You know what I mean."

You need to bring everything
to the table.

I knew exactly what he meant. He sensed I was wise to body language and idiosyncrasies. I could read a room and understand the silent cues, see the hidden agendas, know what was important to others, and communicate in their language. In shorter terms, Mark could sense that I had street smarts, and encouraged me to leverage that skill.

Mark encouraged me to bring more "me" to work, and I learned to lean into it. Not quite Bruce Wayne but definitely more will, more skill, and more betting big on myself. Mark knew I could read a room, understand people, drill down to or distill the facts. He wanted me to bring more "dollar out of 15 cents types of ideas." More creativity to work. I did, and we were successful at nearly every opportunity.

Never Give Up

THERE ARE A LOT OF DIFFERENT ASPECTS of data centers: security, connectivity, and all sorts of safety systems. However, the one aspect that rules supreme is power. Power redundancy and power diversity are critical, but nothing supersedes the importance of how accurately audited that power is. If power auditing is not built into the actual infrastructure of the data center, then it can be become very expensive and labor-intensive to mechanize at any capacity.

The challenge with auditing data centers is that you literally have hundreds of thousands of circuit breakers throughout a data center. Getting an audit of all of that can be incredibly difficult, not to mention time-consuming. The data center I operated had individual circuit-level monitoring, but you had to take a reading on each circuit one at a time. And readings could only be performed at night. Well, I had another macro idea. By working with a vendor, I was able to create an on-demand script (sequence of technical tasks) that would enable us to automatically update all the branch circuit levels with accurate power readings in 15 minutes. For context, this task carried a 7-day turnaround time on a few dozen to a few hundred circuit breakers. Updating hundreds of thousands was not even possible until we created that script.

After figuring out how to get the script created for free, our data center became the most accurately audited data center in the company (worldwide). This was largely because we could update our power readings across the entire data center every 15 minutes (back in 2009). With this victory, I began to feel more confident about what I could accomplish. This confidence grew from a combination of the macros I created as a non-management employee working in my first role, creating the simulators in my previous role, the fast memory recall and application of a Justice League cartoon in the successful interview, and this new power-auditing automation. The concept of building on what I had already learned was something I realized I was good at. Recalling details from a long time ago or enhancing solutions I had already created and modifying them to fit new challenges was now becoming a strategic advantage.

One day, I was invited to a meeting with one of our largest clients, an airline company that had a footprint of several thousand square feet. At some point, all of the data center employees had performed work in their environment, so being invited to that meeting was nothing new. I mean, it was a little different because there were more people participating than normal, but it was all good. Now, this particular company had a very laid-back dress code. Most of the time, they would wear shorts and T-shirts. During this one particular meeting, there might've been seven or eight of the airline employees, plus three or four folks from AT&T sales, Mireya (another data center manager), and me (in suit and tie).

One guy from the airline joked, "David, I'm gonna get you a short set." In jest, he would often joke and give me a hard time for wearing a suit to the data center.

As we got into the meeting, the customer began talking about a large project they wanted to start soon. The project required a bunch of specialized equipment we would have to order, which meant it was going to have an elongated lead time.

After about 15 minutes of discussion, I interrupted the conversation. I said, "This sounds like it's something that you guys are really serious about. I trust you truly want to move forward with this work and digital expansion. If so, please send me the specifics. I will place the orders now, so we'll have the equipment and supplies on-site. This will cut the lead time dramatically. Therefore, when you're ready to pull the trigger, it'll take us two or three days instead of two or three months. Cool?"

I looked around at the stunned faces, waiting a few seconds before moving straight on.

"Great. OK, I gotta go back to work. Just send the specifics, and I'll place the order."

Then I left the meeting.

Typically, this wasn't the process. There were all sorts of approvals to spend funding before customers are ready to buy, but I had saved so much money with other efforts that my funding source trusted me completely. I made good on my commitment and ordered the special equipment in advance, so the actual project work only lasted two to three days. Later, I found out that their executive vice president and a couple other senior VPs were also in the aforementioned meeting... wearing shorts and T-shirts. The way I found out was surprising. The airline's leadership sent a note saying that they decided to renew a multimillion-dollar contract with a first right of refusal (worth even more multi-millions of dollars) without going to RFP (request for pricing, where customers are shopping for the best deal). This was predominantly based on their confidence in me to manage their environment. Soon after, I started receiving congratulatory notes and emails.

Not long after this contract was signed, my mentor, Rick Resnick, invited me to have a meeting with him. Rick was one of the youngest officers in the company. Another mentor of mine, Paula Day Caldwell, reported to

Rick. Paula was a VP and the first person to critique my résumé (back when I worked in tech support). When she did, she red-inked both sides of the page, even though my résumé was a one-pager at the time. After making all the edits she recommended, I was left with only about a paragraph.

Upon reviewing the edits, I said to Paula, "I don't think I need to look for a job. I think I need to look for more accomplishments to put on my résumé."

"I think you and I are going to get along just fine," she said, a grin spreading across her face.

The 37th Floor

AFTER THE BIG AIRLINE DEAL, I had a meeting with Rick, followed by a meeting with Paula, after which I landed myself a promotion in 2010 as a second line manager, a service executive on the business side of AT&T. It was an amazing opportunity, but it was not for the faint of heart. You might know how this scenario plays out: you're the new person on the team, and you get the "more challenging" work to see what you're really made of. (See also: you get assigned the accounts that require more effort.) Yeah, that's precisely what happened here. I was assigned two accounts. One was a large Fortune 500 company that was a household name for personal computers that had recently had a multi-day outage. I also inherited an online travel company that had recently had a multi-hour outage.

You can probably imagine that these companies were not too happy at the time, but it didn't matter to me. That was the past. I was going to own this relationship and turn it around. In order to have conference calls during the daytime hours with my colleagues in the European region, I worked crazy hours in the middle of the night. Some nights, when my teenage son was restless, I would let him hear these off-hour European calls, so he could hopefully absorb an important lesson.

"Son, your competition will not live in the same country as you. The man I'm talking to halfway around the world is telling his son the same thing I'm telling you, which is to do better than I am. You hear this guy? He speaks three languages and has a double degree in Computer Science and Economics. His son will be your competition."

Indeed, the competition was real. However, I knew I was cut out for it. Long story short, both of those companies completely turned around under my leadership and thus rewarded us with perfect customer experience scores. The personal computer company increased their revenue spend with us by 51 percent. Annually, this was worth eight digits left of the decimal point in extra/incremental (or, as I would call it, *exponential*) revenue. Oh, and the online travel company purchased and installed one of the first business voice-over IP systems in our firm.

There was a very critical executive meeting that Rick, my senior VP, had with his peer, a lady named Dolly, at the online travel company. Dolly was known for being very knowledgeable about the technical details and specific issues that might be impeding her operations. Dolly was well-respected and personally knew many of the people in her organization. During that meeting, Dolly expressed that she shook the trees, and no one had any negative issues with our network or technology. Rick was elated. The meeting went better than expected, and that year, I was number one in the organization. I was working on additional things as well, like driving digital adoption before it became a common practice.

Well, maybe six months into the service executive role, there was a reorganization within our department. Paula was moved to a different territory, and my director changed. My new supervisor was Lisa Bradford, a Black female. Lisa and I met once, a few months prior, at an AT&T event. We sat at the same table and talked shop a little bit, and we both found out we had a common mentor we both admired named Mike Hamilton.

Unfortunately, cancer claimed Mike's life all too early. So, when Lisa transferred to Dallas from California, I was a familiar face. Lisa was a tough cookie. She knew her stuff. She knew the networks, the network topology, and the associated processes. She knew how it all worked together. She knew the right players, the right stakeholders, and the naysayers, too. You couldn't bullshit Lisa. She taught me valuable lessons in corporate politics.

At one point while working for Lisa, I was trying to get a process changed. My goal was to drive more digital adoption of our billing services so customers would call less. I needed one adjacent group to do a little more work.

In return, I offered to double the adoption rate across the entire business unit. I garnered the support of Lisa and two VPs; however, the VP who sat at the top of the group in question didn't agree with my proposal. As the lowest ranking member in that meeting, I wasn't in a position to push the issue. Lisa knew how passionate I was about it, so she instant messaged me during the meeting, giving me hints and tidbits. She advised I let it go. And in real-time, I did. That day, Lisa taught me a valuable lesson: when to fight for what's right and when to save the fight for another day.

> You've gotta know when to fight
> for what's right, and when to save
> the fight for another day.

Ironically, the following January, Digital First (the concept of digital billing and digital ordering) became our company's number-two priority, just behind driving an effortless customer experience. Even if you change directions, never give up on something you believe is right.

As a service executive, the name of the game was to keep issues from getting to your manager. If you could do that, you were doing well. The better you did that, the better you were resolving issues without further escalation. Beyond that, if you could change a process or fix something for the organization, even better. That's where I was at. I would not allow anything to escalate beyond myself, and I was working on things to solve processes for the broader organization.

A few months into the service executive role, the company started a program called LWD, which stood for Leading with Distinction. In this program, each of the direct reports to the chairman would provide a leadership presentation. AT&T Headquarters is in Dallas. By living in Dallas, if you attended these sessions in person, you had access to nearly all the direct reports of the chairman. It was a tremendous opportunity to have a program where local employees could be in the same room with the executive leadership team. Now, let me remind you, Lisa was tough. She didn't play any games. That meant that for me to be able to spend time going to these events in person, I had to have my account issues resolved.

Well, I had my accounts under control. In fact, they were growing in revenue. So, I attended nearly all the LWD presentations in person. At the end of each session, there would be a Q&A session, and wouldn't you know it, the same thing seemed to happen every time. After they started the Q&A session, the room went silent, and very few people were quickly asking a question. I knew that was my opportunity. So, I began to prepare questions to ask at each presentation. I made sure my questions were short, thought-provoking for the audience, and relevant in topic so the leader could knock it out of the park. Did I mention the questions I asked were short? Another lesson I've learned is in open settings like these, it's best to be bold, be brief, and be gone.

In these situations, it's best to be bold, be brief, and be gone.

When I asked a question during the first few LWD sessions, they would address me, "Yes, the gentleman in the back has a question." A few months later, that turned into, "Yes, David. Do you have a question?" As a second-level manager, to be promoted to director, you would need the approval of a direct report to the chairman. Well, now they all knew who I was and knew I had a firm understanding of the business.

One day, I was leaving the auditorium after one of those LWD sessions. About five of us piled into the elevator bay at the concourse (underground) level, including Dr. Bill Blasé, our HR leader and former mentor of mine, Larry Solomon, our corporate PR leader (also a supporter of mine), and our CEO and chairman, Randall Stephenson. They were going to the top floor, which was the 37th, and I was going to the first floor to cross the street where I worked in building three on the seventh floor.

Thinking quickly, I struck up a conversation. I said, "You know I work on the 37th floor too, but I've never seen you guys in the mailroom."

Confused, they all looked at each other and then at me.

I said, "Building Three, seventh floor."

We all had a quick laugh, and I exited.

The next day, I was on my way home from work. It was getting a little dark, as I was working late that day. I often worked until the lights turned off in the building. I'm not saying that's the only way or the best way to get things done, but sometimes it just is what it is. That said, at the time, I was in the drive-through at Taco Bueno. I worked at Taco Bueno during my senior year in high school. I loved the fact that the food was fresh and mostly all handmade. While I was in the drive-through, I received a call from my supervisor, Lisa Bradford.

Lisa said, "David, are you sitting down? Because I have good news. Our chairman and CEO wants to have a one-on-one meeting with you."

Now, remember, the chairman was one of the men in the elevator—Randall.

I was too excited to contain myself and immediately yelled, "Yes!"

Meeting with the chairman is like meeting with the president of the United States. There were eight meetings leading up to the meeting and several debriefing meetings afterward. They wanted to know what I was going to talk about at 2:00, at 2:02, at 2:06, and at 2:12. On many levels, it was *meticulous*. This meeting that Randall wanted to have was starting a company-wide initiative called Not So

Undercover Boss. Similar to the TV show "Undercover Boss", the senior executive would spend time with the employee, but in this initiative, it wasn't a surprise. The employee was aware that it was an executive shadowing them. I learned that Randall is the kind of leader to actively lead. So logically, if he could make the time, then his executive team could do the same, and hence a company-wide initiative would be launched.

There's a passage in the Bible that speaks about Moses going into the innermost of the temple and talking to God. When he did so, a cloud would form inside the temple. God spoke to Moses through that cloud, and they would speak like two friends. Well, the Bible also says that God is the same yesterday and today. So, anytime it rains or is cloudy, I look at it a little differently and suppose God is making a special appearance to have a conversation with a friend in need.

The day of the meeting, it was misting just a little bit. So, instead of our chairman walking across the street, he was escorted underground, where I was set to meet him. Together, we were going to walk through the concourse and skywalk to get to my building/cubicle.

As we were approaching the first set of elevator bays, I could see a friend of mine, Cherie Pearson, walking into the elevator. She was several steps ahead of us.

I called out to her. "Cherie, would you hold the elevator, please?"

She did, and much to her surprise, I stepped on the elevator with the man of the hour, our chairman. I introduced the two of them, and Randall asked how she was doing. She was honest and told him she wasn't doing too good—she had just received some tough news. Randall said he hoped that she would feel much better, and then we continued our journey. (I later found out that Cherie had received a letter indicating that she was to be laid off.)

Later that day, she sent a note to Randall explaining her situation, and he found her a role working on a highly prioritized effort in IT. Being in the front row to witness something amazing like that was a major blessing. Cherie later told me that she was trying to hurry up and get on the elevator before us because she didn't want to see me. She didn't want to talk about the fact that she was going to be surplused.

She knew I was going to ask her how she was doing, and of course, she didn't want to share at the time.

And this is where believers say, "Won't He do it."

After that elevator conversation with Cherie, we made our way over to building three and onto the seventh floor, where Randall had one meeting scheduled before mine. It was a Not So Undercover Boss session with someone from a different organization. From my understanding, that session lasted about an hour and a half and didn't go so well. During this time, all the plans that I had previously scheduled were abruptly canceled.

Now, the last thing I wanted was for the chairman to visit with me while I had nothing to do. Not a good look at all. However, what did happen was something like a fire drill. There was an outage the night before that one of my large customers experienced at a key location. You could say this would have been a good time to panic, but I didn't. I remembered how I had remained calm in other make-or-break situations, like when the jack tilted and the car fell while I was under it. This was another do-or-die moment, and I knew God hadn't brought me this far just to give up now.

After Randall's first meeting, he walked over, took a seat in my cubicle, and we got right to it. He watched me deal with outages and critical customer resolution, including billing issues, technical problems, and other sorts of issues that came up and were resolved in real-time. For nearly four hours, he got to see it all. He also had a chance to watch the account team strategize over something that I felt was our secret weapon. That product was called Wireless Backup, and my personal belief was that this product had the most amazing value proposition… and still does.

There used to be a belief that companies thought they had a better network if half of their network was with one telecom provider while the other half of their network was with another telecom provider. In theory, it didn't sound too bad. But in actuality, it was a pain in the neck because neither provider would give a full view of what their network looked like so you could overlay it with the other. Therefore, it worked a whole lot better if all of the network was through one company, so you could look at the entire network topology of the circuit design. With Wireless Backup, if there was a loss of connection on the primary or wireline connection, then a wireless connection would automatically connect to keep the business running. Plus, a lot of companies would run their branch divisions, satellite locations, and/or some of their retail locations on consumer-based broadband.

Although low-cost internet made economic sense, if that connection failed or there was an outage, it would be rough to get through. Having a wireless connection that the store could fail-over to if the primary internet went down is what would reduce the impact of the outage. One of the customers I was supporting at the time was a very large pizza company. It had tens of thousands of locations and broadband endpoints. They recently had an outage at one of their busiest stores, and the issue was escalated to their CIO (Chief Information Officer). We resolved the issue by the following morning, but questions remained. What could be done to prevent this? What do we do if this happens again?

I wholeheartedly believed that Wireless Backup was the correct solution. Randall was there to hear this strategic discussion, in which he heard me take something that was a negative and turn it into a positive. He understood how the solution could be broadly used to increase wireless net adds (sales), strengthen the resiliency of our wireline network, and provide an experience to customers that very few companies have the capabilities to provide. What company in the United States can you buy internet from that automatically switches over to their wireless network if it fails? And then once the primary internet is restored, switches back over to the primary? You let me know.

Randall was thoroughly impressed. And in our nearly four hours together, he took over four pages of notes.

He said, "David, I want you to follow up with me once you've figured the Wireless Backup deal out. Sound good?"

I was elated. "I most certainly will, sir."

Later, as I walked him to the lobby as he was leaving for the day, I felt this was my window to shoot my shot. "Randall, I'd love the opportunity to shadow and learn how you are able to move strategically at a macro level."

"I've had a few young, bright people ask me something similar, but I haven't quite figured out a way to make that happen because a lot of my work is confidential," he said.

I was aware that CEOs typically spent about 70 percent of the time away from the company, so, when he said this, I didn't take it as a surprise. I just thanked him for his time.

Show Me the Money

NOT LONG AFTER THE MEETING with our chairman, the good Lord sent me a blessing in the form of a job opening for a director role in the customer experience organization. A couple of days later, I spoke with my supervisor, Lisa Bradford, during one of our one-on-one meetings. We met regularly so I could update her on the status of my accounts and address any topics on my mind. At the time, I had a module of four accounts that brought in a little north of $120 million annually. As you might imagine, the conversations were always meaningful, but this particular meeting was destined to be different.

When I arrived at Lisa's office, she waved me in, and I closed the door behind me. To offer some perspective about my role, the most important metric (other than revenue) is the experience rating of these high-valued Fortune 500 Enterprise customers regarding their relationship with our company. Every aspect of the account goes into the rating, like sales, orders, circuits, downtime, outages, billing, new technology, and more. All those accounts have global footprints, so if something went wrong halfway around the world, it was my responsibility to get it resolved with as little effort or impact as possible on the customer. Hence why I would have 2 a.m. conference calls with the Europe team. At the time, all my accounts had rated our relationship a perfect 10 out of 10.

With this in mind, I started the meeting by saying, "Lisa, I need to ask you for a favor."

She was typing away, multi-tasking as usual. Her computer faced adjacent to me, so she casually turned her head to the side and said, "Okay, sure. What's up?" while she proceeded to keep typing.

I said, "Well, it's kind of a big favor."

She responded, "Alright, David. What's up?"

I said, "I'm going to need you to say yes *before* I ask."

She stopped typing, turned to me, and sternly said, "What have you done?"

I smiled and replied, "There is a director role that I'm interviewing for, and the hiring manager may reach out to you. When they do, I need you to proactively stand on your desk and shout from the rafters that I am the best candidate for the job and tell them that they need not interview anyone else. And if you don't feel confident in doing so, could you please let me know what it is I could work on so that you *do* feel confident to do so?"

Lisa thought about it for a minute. She flashed a mischievous smile, nodded her head, and said, "Sure, David. I gotcha."

The hiring manager, Lisa Brewer, was from New Jersey. She sent a note to my supervisor while she was out on vacation. On her day off, Lisa Bradford replied to Lisa Brewer with a seven-paragraph letter of recommendation. *That* is true leadership and sponsorship. Now, Lisa's endorsement didn't come cheap for me, either. When she took her vacation, I covered all escalations and accounts. Any time there was an issue with one of those accounts, whether in the middle of the night or on a weekend, Lisa called me, and I engaged. Lisa was preparing me to be able to handle the responsibility of solving unsolvable issues *and* providing me the opportunity to show myself that I could do this.

There were a lot of lessons I learned from my time with Lisa. Most importantly, I learned what it's like to really have a supporter—someone you don't have to guess whether they are really on your side and working on your behalf. When you find yourself in a productive work arrangement, don't waste a single day. Learn, grow, partner, listen, speak up, and contribute like there's no tomorrow. It will pay dividends. There are no traffic jams on the extra mile, and that's where the true top performers can be found. The more steps in faith you take, the closer you are to your stride. Lisa is a master at politics, and I learned all

I could from her. She encouraged me to do my best and never dim my light. She expected much, but when much was delivered, much was given. If you find yourself in a situation where your efforts are not being reciprocated, remember that we generally don't have the power or the right to change anyone. Identify, communicate, evaluate, adapt, and move forward. Your purpose is much larger than any singular issue you may encounter. Don't lose sight of your courageous purpose or unique business model you are here to introduce unto the world. Stay focused.

There are no traffic jams
on the extra mile.

I prepped for the director interview like my life depended on it. I aggregated a binder full of information and canvassed people who were close to that organization. When it was time for the interview, I actually flew to New Jersey on my own dime. What I didn't know was that the hiring manager had to fly to Atlanta on an unexpected but necessary trip. So, the interview ended up being on the phone. *No worries.* I had a Bluetooth in my ear, and all the information from the binder laid out page by page around the edge of the hotel bed so I wouldn't have to flip through them. I just walked around the bed to read all the pages I laid out.

The interview with Lisa Brewer went great. After the interview, I emailed her a copy of my digital Prezi portfolio.

Later, I interviewed with a woman named Brenda Kittila, who was also a vice president in the customer experience organization. That interview went well. Lastly, I interviewed with the senior vice president. During that interview it "felt" like he had just received a copy of my résumé and randomly picked one bullet from the page to discuss. In all transparency, it wasn't my best bullet. It wasn't bad, but it wasn't my best. That said, I was well prepared and tremendously grateful for these opportunities. God knows it was an answered prayer. I was also very committed to being the very best I could be in every situation. Not for the sake of being number one, but rather because I believed I could make a meaningful difference.

It took a while, but I got the job and was promoted to director. This promotion put me in the top 4 percent of the company, and excited was an understatement. I had gone from non-management to director in less than four years. And I was on a roll, too. As I headed? to a new exciting part of the company, I also had been awarded my first patent, and was energized to make a difference.

You Had Me at Hello

AS A DIRECTOR, the first thing I worked on was competitive intelligence. I walked around with a Verizon, T-Mobile, and Sprint phone in my pocket every day. I visited their stores. I called their call centers. I knew a ton about them and respected their companies. When some thought that T-Mobile was crazy for their commercials and their CEO's Twitter battles, I knew they were up to something genius. Soon after beginning that role, I was awarded my second patent as a director. This patent connected satellite and LTE technology together in what I called a Dual Connectivity Wi-Fi Router. That's right, a DCW router.

Not long after, I also won a Champion of Diversity award from Chairman Randall Stephenson and Chief Diversity Officer Corey Anthony. I was on a roll, and I was getting things done. I partnered with a couple of folks and invented intelligent hyperlinks we could use in many different channels. The links were smart enough to recognize what type of device you had and whether or not our native app was installed, then direct you to the appropriate experience based on that device or app. The link would also send you to the appropriate app store or to the native app (if present on the device). Then, once you authenticated through that app, the intelligent link would direct you to a specific page within the app. We built this out to the Nth degree. Before long, we could redirect you to nearly any page within the app (payment, change rate plan, etc.) with one tap or click.

This effort became wildly successful. Last time I checked, we were getting about 100 million impressions a month, which identified opportunities and led teams to drive tens of millions of dollars of benefit. However, I didn't stop there. I partnered with equipment groups to transition from microcells to Wi-Fi, which drove tens of millions in cost savings, and helped pioneer new capabilities like IVR-to-chat through the native mobile app. Throughout this process, I moved laterally as a director four times.

During one of those roles, I started a sales program in a technical organization. *Wait, what?* The first year, the program generated tens of millions of dollars of revenue by leveraging the insight of our mobility tech team and equipping them with a sales offer they were perfectly positioned to sell. I also had multiple one-on-one meetings with two executives, John Stankey (chief strategy officer at the time) and John Donovan (chief technology officer at the time). Sure, these leaders had meetings all the time. However, they were typically not meeting with someone several levels from the C-Suite. I wasn't in any special program and had no sponsor facilitating or introducing me. I wasn't a part of their organization, either. This was just a straight line between the two of us: let's meet. And yes, these moments did feel Rudolph-ish. Both Donovan and Stankey eventually rose to become CEOs. Donovan became CEO of AT&T Communications, while Stankey became CEO of AT&T Inc.

And just to put some things into perspective, folks like Stankey and Donovan seem to be able to see around corners, much like Chairman Randall. I remember the January after Randall became CEO in 2007, he spoke at a press conference. In the Q&A session, someone asked Randall about his outlook on the economy for the current year.

"I think that housing may decline," he said confidently.

There was an audible gasp from the audience. It was almost as if you could hear them saying, "Housing? Housing has appreciated for the last 39 years."

Eerily, our stock price took a small dip after that meeting. At the end of the day, CEOs are graded on their stock price. There's no better indicator of success. So, as a new CEO, I imagine that had to hurt. Especially when you consider that each penny of our stock is worth about $100 million. That said, Randall, being Randall, just carried on doing what he believed was the right thing. In July 2008, he sold all of our company's real estate. It was around a

$3 billion transaction, and, at the time, I believe we were the second-largest real estate owner in the continental United States (excluding the Roman Catholic Church and the federal government). A few months after the sale, in September, the housing market crashed. I also heard we yielded three times the value from that transaction than what we could've garnered in October.

Remember how I said it seemed like they could see around corners? It must be a CEO thing.

Stankey is an operator's operator. A lot of the technology advances that we made as a company, including transitioning from wireline to a mobility network, were led by Stankey. He introduced our firm to user-based targeted advertising, and he's been in and led just about every component of our company—earning him the respect of a lot of people. Stankey even led the relocation of our headquarters to Dallas, Texas. Back before it was cool, he was working on network topologies like combining coax and twisted pair to deliver high bandwidth data transmissions. Stankey understands leadership, but he also deeply understands the technology. That's a hard combination to find, let alone beat.

Donovan, on the other hand, ran the largest arm of Verisign before joining AT&T as CTO. He started a six-year budget outlook for the company because what we needed to do couldn't be forecasted in one-year increments. That paved the way for us to prepare one of the largest networks on earth to be videocentric, complete with heat maps to identify problematic areas of the network, separating hardware from the software to drive flexibility, and amazing cost structure. Donovan is a visionary. He started tSpace, an internal social media platform for employees, and initiated both the AT&T Believes and Dream in Black programs, which both directly help people from my community.

Look, you just don't get multiple one-on-one, in-person, hour-long meetings with leaders like that unless you really have something valuable to talk about. However, when you have meetings and build relationships with folks that high in the chain of command, you are certainly going to develop enemies. Some folks are pissed because it happened. In fact, if you dare mention you have any personal connection or a relationship to leaders that high, it could be the career kiss of death. Feeling a little damned-if-you-do and damned-if-you-don't? Join the crowd. We're out of chairs, so be prepared to stand... stand *out*, that is.

Join the crowd. We're out of chairs,
so be prepared to stand...
stand *out*, that is.

My ask of every CEO is to keep this point in their peripheral. You don't need to ask your attaché *if* this is happening in your company. The answer is yes, regardless of what the person(s) who clawed their way to your side says. That said, if people you've mentored are impressive enough to garner your attention, make the effort to keep an open door with them. It's a jungle... no, it's a *swamp* out there.

When I wasn't spending time with the C-Suite, I was killing it in the various director roles. My first director role was in Customer Experience before moving over to become director chief of staff of all AT&T Customer Service, consumer *and* business. Afterward, I moved into social media, chat, and advanced tech. Then I returned to business solutions.

In all these units, I was selected four separate times to be in the high potential distinction, which is the top 10 percent of directors. I was also selected to be in the Accelerated Development Program (ADP), where the top 10 percent of Hi-Potential leaders are chosen. Twice, I was selected into the Black Men Xcel program, as well as the Mid-Level Symposium (MDLS) program. And then, the following year, I was sponsored in the CALIBR program, which is a continuation of MDLS. I also won a Dream in Black award the inaugural year. It's awarded annually to 28 individuals across a company of 250,000 for their work in the communities to improve engagement, equity, and inclusion.

But back to where we were.

In 2017, I had a Jerry Maguire moment. I was working for Dr. Ron Hyland, a true friend and profound leader in running operations, when I came up with an idea. Ron led social media, chat, and advanced tech at the time. To keep things proprietary, I'll stay high-level and just say this—what I invented is something called Credit Decision Engine (CDE). I pursued funding for a year, and finally, my mentor, Mo Katibeh, was able to assist in securing funding of roughly $6 million. We deployed the solution the first year and yielded $119 million year-over-year improvement. The following year yielded $175 million on top of that. Mo had similar successes early in his career, even before he moved up the chain of command. I learned from Mo that if you have a really good idea that you truly believe in, keep taking it higher and higher until you reach a level where the value of the effort can be assessed minus any political headwinds.

Jerry Maguire is one of my favorite movies. I love the "show me the money" and "you had me at hello" scenes. CDE was both.

Now, before I move on, there is no way I could talk about that project and not mention a few super friends that helped to bring it to fruition: Tamora Burns, Bryan Welker, Christine Phan, Sukanta Nanda, and Sachin Kulkarni. Thank you.

A Long Way
from South Dallas

IT WAS 2012 when I moved into the newly formed Customer Service organization. That group was intended to be a tip of the spear type of department that would perform and review research internally and externally. We looked for trends to identify pain points, points of failure, and areas of opportunity to reduce friction among those serving our customers so that we could provide and deliver an effortless customer experience.

In this organization, one of the things that we were ultimately measured on was net promoter score (NPS). Net promoter score is how many promoters of your service or product you have, divided by how many detractors of that same product or service and the percentage thereof. With a company our size, at the time, one percentage point of net promoter score was valued at over nine digits left of the decimal. It was our chairman's number one priority, and it truly was a big deal.

Our leader and senior vice president, John Dwyer, invited the directors and above to a strategy session in Atlanta, Georgia. It lasted for a few days and was incredibly productive. There was a ton of knowledge sharing between the consultants and our firm. Throughout the meetings, I noticed there was one gentleman there who sat near the back of the room and listened. Near the end of the three-day session, he finally spoke. It was strange because when this guy started talking, he immediately reminded me of one of my oldest friends, Trayl. I could tell that the guy was not only smart, but he was also patient and wise. He almost seemed to instinctively know what every person in the room was thinking. It was amazing to watch.

Not only did I feel smarter just because I was in the room with him, but I also felt like it *mattered* that I was in the room with him. And he made everyone in the room feel that way. The man I speak of is John Stupka, former CEO of Southwestern Bell Mobile Systems, former president of Skytel Pagers, and former right-hand man to Ralph de la Vega, CEO of AT&T Mobility and Business Solutions.

Ralph, a Cuban American consummate professional, was later promoted and retired as vice chairman of AT&T. He beat the competition nearly every quarter he held the office. Officially, Stupka was a contractor. Also, officially, Stupka was the truth. He only worked on huge efforts. Issues that had no solution in sight were his specialty. At the time, I had no prior insight into who Stupka was. I just knew that the person who was talking in the room was someone I wanted to learn from for years to come.

Officially, Stupka was a contractor.
Also, officially, Stupka was the truth.

My supervisor, Lisa Brewer, had already planned what my first assignment would be—an extensive exercise in competitive intelligence. My research, combined with Lisa's leadership, led to a few large initiatives, one being a deeper discount on mobility products for our employees. Working for Lisa, I was fortunate to witness firsthand what it meant to simultaneously be a trendsetter, a scrappy hustler, and an executive. As you might remember, this was the second Lisa I had worked for and also the second Lisa who challenged me and pushed me to be better. This was also not the last Lisa I would report to.

After completing the first major Competitive Intelligence assignment, I was presented with another one. The assignment was an exercise that fell somewhere between science and art, deploying a holistic profile of a customer called the Snapshot tool. This profile was built almost completely from feedback from our customer-facing employees, and it was Lisa and John's brainchild. It was genius. It was a tool that was two pages deep, required very little navigation, and had over 200 data points about the customer, all presented in a crisp and vivid display. Once the development was done and testing was complete, it was time to roll out the new application across 60,000 customer-facing employees in the centers and stores. However, before we moved all of heaven and earth to do so, we rolled this application out in one call center, learned a few lessons, modified the rollout strategy, and then scaled. This tool was called Customer Snapshot.

My role in this exercise of technology and execution was to launch the new application in the Tulsa, Oklahoma, call center, identify what was needed to deliver strong results quickly, and then scale the effort across all of customer service. It was around this time that I started reminding myself that I used to catch the 44 Oakland city bus from Val's Liquor Store on Bexar Street to go to Saint Anthony. I was just trying to make a way out of no way when I started selling candy at school.

> I was just trying to make a way
> out of no way when I started
> selling candy at school.

Here I was, the same guy, yet I was a *long* way from South Dallas.

OK, let's keep going.

I set up a plan to execute the rollout in the Tulsa call center and shared a copy with Lisa. She provided a few edits, which I incorporated into the rollout strategy. Once

Lisa and I were both pleased with the plan, it was time to execute. Shortly thereafter, I received a call from Stupka. He wanted to meet at the Starbucks in the lobby of our headquarters building, Whitaker Tower. I also worked in Whitaker Tower on a different floor, so I was able to meet at the Starbucks right away.

The beginning of the discussion started off casual, with Stupka asking me questions about my family and my son. He also had a son and was very proud of him as well. He shared that in parenting, you never really know if you got it right until your child has a child. Then you get to really discover if what you taught was truly retained. He was a very wise man indeed.

After the pleasantries, he dove into the topic at hand. "Lisa and I have talked, and I believe you're going to do an absolutely phenomenal job in Tulsa. As I understand it, David, that's all you know how to do. You have an impressive track record. Let's talk about your plan for the rollout."

What a way to start a conversation! I was excited for the mission at hand and walked through the plan with him. Stupka listened before offering a suggestion and an objective. His suggestion came in the form of a question.

"Do you think you have enough goodies?"

Goodies were prizes for the Tulsa agents, and what this question really meant was that he felt like I could use a few more incentives and prizes to drive more productivity. I agreed with him, and he said he would take care of it.

Then he moved on to his expectations, which were very clear and non-numerical.

He said, "David, your goal is not to force the agents to use the new tool, and your measure of success will not be a number on a chart. Your goal is to master the art of the possible. Imagine one agent sitting down in a breakroom next to another, asking, 'Hey, have you tried that new Snapshot tool?' If the response was no, then you would want the first agent to respond, 'Well, I just don't see why not.'"

Now, let me remind you, this was the first time that Stupka and I had a one-on-one conversation. And in very short order, he inspired me to aspire to a higher level of greatness. Thankfully, this would also not be the last time.

There are very few business problems I've been asked to solve that didn't result in costs lower than expected, results higher than forecasted, and teams happier than ever. However, Stupka (and Lisa) still challenged me.

> There are very few business problems
> I've been asked to solve
> that didn't result in costs lower
> than expected, results higher
> than forecasted, and teams
> happier than ever.

After a five-hour drive north to Tulsa, I approached the facility, and something out of this world happened. Not

100 yards away from the building was this huge billboard. It's important to note here that the building and the billboard both faced the highway. A familiar face was on the billboard, a friend who, early in her career, was asked to take pictures that would be used in AT&T collateral. I remembered when the company first started employee-centric marketing because I also participated. At the time, employees who participated in that effort thought that, at best, our picture might wind up on an internal site. Little did my friend, LaKendra Davis, know that she would be featured on a billboard on a busy highway in Tulsa. At the time that picture was taken, LaKendra might have been a first-line manager. Now she's vice president at a Fortune 100 telecommunications giant.

Won't He do it.

Then came Team Tulsa. From the first time I met the leaders and employees of the Tulsa center, I was greeted with a warm welcome, and the hospitality never ended. The site leader and director, Matt Linden, was the best business partner one could ever hope for. Truly great people have no issue setting politics, ego, and title aside for a common goal and the greater good, and Matt was exactly that. I also remember an employee named Dallas who worked there. Hey, who doesn't love a great name like Dallas? Dallas had pink hair, but her methodologies, skills, and logic were all black and white. Often, Dallas was asked to move around the center and help coworkers who might be struggling with a difficult scenario. Dallas was great at helping individuals embrace the new technology. I realized that with Dallas on board, the rest of the center would surely follow.

Matt, my friend to the end, truly rolled out the red carpet for me. He even invited me to participate in his town hall meetings and brought me up every time he took the stage. He was completely committed to setting the pace of adoption and operational excellence for the entire organization. What we collectively accomplished together did just that. After a couple weeks, the results were in, and the trends were holding. We reduced average call time by more than 30 seconds, and our experience scores improved by four percentage points. During the four-week launch, Stupka was so pleased that he traveled to Tulsa to see the good news for himself and lend his support. When we both returned to Dallas, he had a lot more waiting for me. However, that wasn't my only surprise.

The day I returned home, I found out that my son's cousin and best friend, Chris, was moving in with us. Chris is a year older than my son, Alex, and works in cybersecurity. When he was just a sophomore in high school, I was fortunate enough to inspire him to pursue a career in computer science. He chose cyber security. We stayed close while he was in college. He has an epic story, including playing NCAA D1 basketball. I pray for Alex and Chris daily.

The Stupka Effect

AS THE YEAR WENT ON, Stupka and I worked on several projects together. It was hard to tell if there was a limit to his brilliance, but one thing that was not hard to tell was that he most certainly knew exactly what he was doing. And if you were smart (and lucky), you joined forces with him and accomplished greatness. For example, one specific effort comes to mind.

Stupka had asked me to pull together some research regarding digital adoption. Once I was done, he looked at the research, made a few edits, and discussed them with me until he was settled on the various topics. Then he erased everything except the column and row headers of the work. *Not exactly what I had in mind before my upcoming meeting with a few VPs.* But Stupka counseled me wisely.

He said, "In a room full of leaders at this level and caliber, it's best to leave the decisions up to them." He advised me that if we were truly right in the way we were thinking about the topic, then through the way that we framed up the slide and the direction of our conversation, we *should* see those leaders come to similar (if not the same) conclusions.

Once again, he was so very right. I would have never taken an approach like that. Never even considered it as an option! I learned a lot from him.

The last project we worked on together was a new business model that I invented for customer service. Stupka loved it, and I was thrilled that I had truly excited him in something novel that we could work on together. This new business model would save 40 to 45 percent OpEx (operational expense) for customer service. He quickly pulled conversations together with our legal team and compliance organization and gained conditional approval. Me being me, I was excited that I had found a 300-million-dollar opportunity. However, Stupka, in his wisdom, uncovered another significant benefit.

He said, "The savings are nice. But the bigger win is that because of this new business model you are introducing, this effort could be an affordable way to bring jobs back stateside, with a higher pay." He knew the bigger win.

Unfortunately, my time with Stupka expired shortly after we started working on this effort together. All the while he was solving some of the largest problems in telecommunications, he was also battling cancer. He beat it once. But the second battle was different. We talked right up until the last week he was here. During our last conversation, he didn't accept defeat, but he did let me know that we may not be able to talk much going forward.

Stupka kept it real. He wouldn't do the Hollywood shuffle. He wouldn't promise you one thing and then do another. He told me of mistakes he made *and* things he was proud of. He loved solving problems, and he loved his ranch. Yet, above all, he loved his wife and children the most.

There are too many lessons I learned from Stupka to name them all, but a few come to mind. He would say that there are three things that will solve almost anything in the world: visibility, accountability, and consequence (good or bad).

Stupka also taught me to love reporting while many overlook or don't care much for it. Some hate putting reports together, and some hate how long it takes to create reports. Then others pick reports apart and find errors. Sadly, reporting teams rarely get the funding they need to advance.

I took that reporting lesson to heart. Some overlooked report often led me to some undiscovered pool of savings. In fact, it was a rarely read weekly report that led me to invent CDE so we could realize a few hundred million dollars in a couple years!

Stupka would say, "It's ironic and frustrating if someone wants to debate who's going to solve problem ABC or

XYZ... because there are so many things to solve. Why are you worried about this solution? If you would study the report, you would find your own pool of savings."

Stupka and I also agreed on the concept of being strategic. If something was strategic, then every iteration would be cheaper and faster. Some might disagree and claim that when you strategically migrate from one technology to another, there's a huge cost that comes with that. Stupka would still say, "Maybe, but still probably no."

Yes, some efforts are expensive, but if you're doing it right, it's only expensive once (if that), not once every five years. Many people believe the automation in Tony Stark's home costs tens of millions of dollars. However, the truth is that an Alexa and about a thousand bucks will get you almost all of what you see in Tony's home in the movie!

As you can see, I learned a lot from Stupka. He will truly be missed.

Trending Now: Miracles

IT'S A GLOBAL FACT that the year 2020 was challenging, to say the very least. However, before that inevitable certainty dawned on the world, there was a challenge that was about to rock *my* whole world. My older sister, Angelia Loria, was diagnosed with cancer—neuroendocrine tumors in her abdomen, to be exact. This is the same cancer that the greats Aretha Franklin and Steve Jobs battled.

My sister, my hero, enlisted in the Air Force right after high school. At the time, I was in the ninth grade, and my mother convinced me to join JROTC (Junior Reserve Officers' Training Corps). Initially, I felt like JROTC wasn't a very cool class to join. Green uniforms and all the military stuff seemed a little weird for high school. However, my mom asked if I would do it for her, so I did. I later grew to love it.

When Angelia was 16 and started to drive, she also worked two jobs while in high school. That inspired me to start working at 14 years old at a grocery store a few miles from home. I would pay for the cab to and from work with the money I earned from tips—that is, until I quit because the manager used my Social Security number for his utilities. But that's a whole 'nother story. Anyways. The point is, I wanted to be like Angelia. She went into the military, and it inspired me to join JROTC. She went to Skyline High School, and that's the only high school I wanted to attend. Her first car was a Chevy Cavalier, and so was mine. My sister being an enlisted soldier during the first Gulf War, Operation Desert Storm, was larger than life to me.

To me, Angelia was perfect. While she was in high school—the age where children often lose their minds—my sister was absolutely nothing like that. She never cut class. She never used drugs. She never got into trouble. All her friends were upstanding and outstanding students in school and very respectable kids in the neighborhood. During her teenage years, she also landed a spot on the Skyline Silhouettes, a prestigious female drill team.

Angelia is six feet tall with long, natural hair. Occasionally, she would press it, but never anything more. Usually, she would wear a single, long, braided ponytail and show off her 360 waves from tip to tip. I'm six years younger than my sister, and I don't think I can recall ever beating her in a foot race. Not as kids *or* adults.

She was always ahead of her time, as if she had been here before. Brilliant and resourceful. In all my life, I don't think I've ever seen her do one person wrong. And when she was diagnosed with cancer, it just seemed so wrong. As you may remember, the day our father committed suicide, Angelia, at 13 years old, held her composure together and led me, her 8-year-old little brother, out of the house so we were safe and my mother could focus on my dad. How could something as horrible as a cancer diagnosis happen to a person like her?! However, when God says He's never seen the righteous forsaken, He is *not* mistaken.

> When God says
> He's never seen the righteous forsaken,
> He is not mistaken.

In February 2020, my sister went to the VA (Veterans Administration) hospital, where she was diagnosed with 39 tumors in her abdomen. It hit me like a ton of bricks. To this day, the gravity of it is very sobering. My sister knows how much I look up to her. She's not perfect, but in so many ways, she *is* what's right in the world.

Now, I've been through some things. As an anomaly, I've been in the valley of the shadow of death. I've seen God move mountains. I've seen Him preparest a table before me in the presence of mine *un*supporters. From the very first time my sister told me about the horrible disease, I said, "Well this ain't the end." I refused to believe anything short of a miracle was about to happen.

Seriously, I know it shocked her to hear me say it so fast—and it definitely took me by surprise—but I just could not see my sister in a casket. I simply couldn't accept that. That wasn't the God I knew, and I *knew* what God could do. I had seen Him educate a little Black boy about business with lessons that would last a lifetime. In high school, all those JROTC championships were nothing short of miracle work. In my late teens, I had seen Him save my life under that car and on that plane. When I fractured my lower spine and was unable to walk, He restored my body. I knew in my heart of hearts that it was not the end for my sister. I knew it would require unwavering faith in God to do His thing and pour us out a blessing in which we did not have room enough to receive. And maybe that's for you today, as you read this. The miracle or blessing is coming, and it's more than you'll be able carry *alone*, so don't forget to share some of that goodness with others.

> The miracle or blessing is coming,
> and it's more than you'll be able
> carry alone, so don't forget to share
> some of that goodness with others.

You know, a surgery to address something like neuroendocrine tumors often carries a cost that has caused many families to ask some difficult financial questions and face horrible circumstances. However, because my sister was a veteran, the bill was already paid. That was the first good sign from the Lord, but that would not be the last.

The next miracle was that the surgeon who performed the operation graduated from Yale.

Are you serious? Nothing against them, but I've heard horror stories about the VA hospital. So, to hear that the surgeon that would be operating on my heroic sister studied at Yale? I had a faith report that showed miracles trending up and confirmation He was about to show out. The surgery lasted for 10 hours, and the results were nothing short of miraculous. All 39 tumors were successfully removed. No chemotherapy needed afterward. No loss of hair. You can't make this stuff up. You also can't allow doubt into the operating room of your life. Sometimes life has some challenges that are created for the sole purpose of taking you to the next level. However, you cannot doubt destiny when you are at the doorstep of your miracle.

We also have to carefully guard our words. I never said or allowed anyone else to say, "Angie's cancer." It was always "that cancer." It wasn't hers.

As an anomaly, there are times when we are faced with a decision to be politically correct or act boldly on the thing in our hearts. And when that idea, notion, or desire is something positive, backed up with what you need to support the vision you are pursuing, then you must have the courage to choose faith over fear. See, the miracle awaiting your life is often cloaked and hidden in fear. This is designed to protect the miracle *just for you*. If you look back, you will see examples of where blessings only intended for you were just beyond the "scary" part. Your past experiences *prove* that your passion to pursue the vision of your life is within reach if we have the faith to boldly reach before (your destiny) is within sight.

Won't He… When He… WIN He Do(es) It.

Passions and Purpose

MY SON, ALEXANDER WILLIAMS, lost his biological father at 5 years old.

Let's put this into perspective. If a loved one has a migraine headache, you can sympathize, but you cannot truly understand what they are going through unless you have personally had a migraine headache. It's a different kind of pain. Ask anyone who's experienced a migraine, and they'll explain.

Relationships are the most powerful thing on this planet, and the bond between a father and son is special, especially when the relationship is nurtured and allowed to connect and grow. Now, losing a parent is a subject with many nuances. To not get too far into the weeds, I'll just say that if you haven't lived that experience as a young child, then you probably will not be able to *fully* understand it. Nothing against any other tragedy. All can be equally rough, but they are also all unique. And so, the unique roughness of this tragedy is the loss of a large, personal, influential, irreplaceable component of who we are at such a tender age. And, to take it a step further, losing a parent in a society where some people are afraid and/or opposed to how nature and history introduced us to the world can leave a young Black child feeling disadvantaged. Stepping into my son's life at that time was a gift from God. I'm grateful to have stepped in during his adolescence, knowing he was going through almost exactly what I went through as well.

My father always stressed the importance of having a healthy appetite for reading, which I've passed along. Alex is an avid reader. At the age of 12, he read Walter Isaacson's biography of Steve Jobs (which is a little north of 600 pages). However, even when it comes to sharing passions and hoping our kids will love what we loved, there are limits as a parent. I was always mindful not to live my life through his. So long as he wanted to be "his" best, it didn't matter what profession, sport, school subject, or class he pursued.

As he was growing up, my approach was to find out what he was good at and support him. Give it your all, and it will pay off. We tried it all—from baseball to piano to football. He later found a love for music, but by eighth-grade mid-terms, football became his focus. It wasn't easy, but he excelled. And when it was time to move on, he did so gracefully.

As he moved into adulthood, we discussed different challenges in his life, and it was through these discussions that I realized part of the reason why I had gone through so many things in my own life. It was so that I could help my son when he had specific life experiences and questions.

When you leverage your past experiences and focus on your true passions, you are operating in your unique business model. Therefore, accomplishing the goal is a by-product. It is nearly automatic. You just need the courage to do what you know is right by God's standards, not yours. It might be scary and unfamiliar, but you *already have* what's needed to accomplish what is before you. All I ever wanted from my father was to be able to ask him questions so I could learn how to navigate through this world without too much heartache.

> When you leverage your past
> experiences and focus on
> your true passions, you are operating
> in your unique business model.

To be there for my son when he needs support, encouragement, and love is amazing. No matter what the topic, it always feels like I am walking in my purpose. God either "lives me" the answer—meaning I've lived something similar that I can draw upon and provide guidance—or I have enough of the answer that Alex needs at *that* time. The rest comes later.

I remember when my son started the ninth grade. We moved to a new neighborhood, and he was trying out for the football team. He was good at football, but he wasn't the fastest player on the team. So, I tried something that I was familiar with when I played football in school. I bought my son a bike and encouraged him to ride the bike to school during the summer on his way to football practice. I knew it would help him with his speed, which would help his confidence and give him some quiet time to think. However, we lived in a really nice neighborhood. Every time he would try to ride his bike to school, one of the neighbors would see him, pull over, pick him up, throw his bike in the back of their truck and drive him to school. Therefore, that particular plan didn't work. The neighbors were too hospitable. All good. Hopefully, no one holds grudges against good neighbors; I certainly don't.

Our past experiences have value. However, they don't always play out in the present as they did in the past. And that's okay. We have to leave room for every new day to have a new opportunity to be something new. Alex was much better in sports than I was. He wound up being selected as the starting junior varsity and varsity quarterback for a couple years. He was happy. I was happy. My only sports goal for him was to learn how to win, how to lose, and how to compete. All the rest was for him. Whether he got faster or not was a much smaller factoid than what type of resiliency and character he was developing.

I mention this because it's important to understand your passion, no matter your age or profession. After identifying your passion, you *must* feed it and nurture it daily. All people and all things love good/plentiful food. Your passion is no exception. All good things can come to an end. If you don't use it, you can lose it. So, look deep inside yourself and find what gets you going. What is something you would do without taking a break? What is something that you would cancel a trip for and not be upset? What is something that you do and lose track of time doing? What do people often look to you for advice on? Or service? The answers to these questions can help you find your professional passion.

After identifying your passion,
you must feed it and nurture it daily.

Pandemic-Level Skill

A FEW WEEKS AFTER MY SISTER'S SURGERY, I had a meeting scheduled with a very senior leader. The in-person meeting had been on the calendar for a couple of months. I had been a director for eight years and had a number of lateral roles that I excelled in. I was on the Hi-Potential list in four different business units, drove hundreds of millions in savings and revenue, was awarded patents, and more.

But I still hadn't been interviewed for advancement.

So, I wanted to discuss what I could do to advance my career and/or pay. The meeting didn't go as expected, but toward the end, I mentioned work from home concept that Stupka and I had worked on about four years prior. The leader advised that I should get some time to pitch the concept to those who led that part of the company.

Later, I sent a note thanking them for their time and sharing documentation from my research. Over the next week, we traded a few emails where they asked questions about getting past potential red-tape items. I provided solid, logical responses to address their concerns until March 13, 2020, when the federal government declared a national emergency due to the outbreak of COVID-19 in the United States. By March 20, the shelter-in-place mandates began. The last note I received from that meeting was in reference to my work from home concept and the rapid state lockdowns.

They said, "Well, I guess we'll see if your theory holds true."

The next week was rough. It became obvious that my concept for working from home was being circumvented by the government's shelter-in-place mandates. I felt like I had this great idea that I had been pitching for years, but now the ideal time had passed to implement the idea. Like, who needs a cutting-edge work from home strategy when the federal government mandates everyone to shelter in place?! It felt like the rug had been pulled out from under me, and my moment of moments had all but slipped away. I was depressed, but God had a different path forward.

To put things into context, at the time, I led an automation team within a sales organization, which means I was a bit of a fish out of water. Although this was a unique configuration, it was not my first time being in a situation like that. (Remember, in my previous role, I started a sales program within a technical organization.) My supervisor at the time was Vice President Trish Renz, and on her weekly staff calls, any open items or pain points of the organization were openly shared and addressed. This is a massive blessing for an automation team. We sat so close to the problem, there was nothing between us and the solution. It was on one of those calls that a few of the leaders started to share the difficulty of our customer-facing and call-taking agents in attempting to facilitate taking a payment or completing a sale while working from home.

We sat so close to the problem,
there was nothing between us
and the solution.

Although the federal government (and the various state governments across the country) mandated that all employees work from home, the telecommunications industry is regulated by the FCC. This agency enforces laws and practices to protect consumers and the general public. One of their rules is that telecommunication employees working from home may not have access to SPI data. SPI data is Sensitive Personal Information, which includes things like date of birth, Social Security number, credit card information, driver's license number, and a few other items.

That was a tough problem. Although so much of our society has converted and committed to digital transactions like payments or purchases, there are millions of people and businesses who call in every month to pay their bills or purchase more products and/or services. Sometimes these callers are not in a setting where they can complete a digital transaction, like a payment or a purchase. Sometimes they have questions associated with the transactions they're requesting. Sometimes they remember their customer service credentials and don't remember their digital credentials. Sometimes the person requesting the transaction is only authorized to perform transactions through customer service and not online. There are several logical reasons why so many transactions still occur in human-assisted channels. So, this was a very big work from home issue. The last thing any company wants to do is impede their ability to take payments or make sales.

Everyone was doing their best to handle the situation as best as they could with the available capabilities. Therefore, we often referred or guided customers to complete their transactions online. We tried to assist them in getting registered online so that they could do so, or we attempted to transfer the customer internally to any agents that might have been working in the call center because their home environment was not conducive to work.

Let's use some round numbers. If 90 percent of the center went home and 10 percent of the employees still needed to work in the center, with payments being a top call type and the whole world trying to connect with smartphones, then you can imagine the bottleneck to reach someone who could complete that payment or sale. The company made accommodations consistent with all of the

CDC guidelines for employees who were unable to work from home to keep working, and we sure did need them because every caller was *not* in an environment where they could go online to complete a payment or purchase more products and services digitally.

Everyone knew that sales were important, but it was a little different at the time. It wasn't just a sale. There were folks that *needed* these products and services. Imagine a medical facility needing to equip their nurses and staff with smartphones and tablets to stay connected and productive during the shelter-in-place mandates. Imagine schools, city utility employees, transportation sectors, a nation of small businesses, and the entire value chain of nearly every industry going mobile and virtual and needing the type of services we provided.

Financially speaking, I wouldn't share any numbers different than what was/is reported publicly in our quarterly earnings reports. Personally speaking, I would say if you have enough punctuation marks to make a sandwich, then whatever you're dealing with is bigger than a bread box. This means that it wasn't lunchtime; it was crunch time. At this time, there were about 40,000 employees being impacted by this rock and hard place scenario in the stores and centers.

It wasn't lunchtime;
it was crunch time.

I Never Run
from Challenges

AT THIS POINT IN MY CAREER, I was leading the largest bot program in the company (and our company has the largest bot program worldwide)—bots as in Robotics Process Automation (RPA). Let me explain. Bots have been around for a long time. They gained a lot of attention several years ago when YouTube and social media started expanding. Some people figured out you could use automated programs to increase views on videos or "clicks" on social media pages. However, the internet has since grown, and most bot-driven traffic has been limited.

But bots didn't end there.

In the corporate world, bots/RPA are still relatively new. However, instead of driving social media or YouTube views, in corporate use-cases, bots perform routine tasks. For example, if you need to perform a massive project of data entry for a million records, a bot can read the form submitted and correctly enter that data into the respective system. The bot can work almost all day long, every day of the year. As if that weren't enough, you can clone the bots so that more work can be performed faster. And finally, the bots never misbehave. No "Terminator" movie stuff. They only do what they are told/programmed to do.

Now, what I just detailed is a very simple use case. There are many more that are much more complex. Many of the bots we build and deploy today solve for some of customer service's most commonly occurring or arduous/difficult tasks.

I started my organization's RPA program in 2018 when I personally completed the training and then recruited others. Training was only a few days and provided very minimal basics of understanding the software, which meant you needed to have some prior understanding of scripting, VBA, Java, C++, or another programming language. You didn't have to be a true coder, but you would certainly need to be able to speak the language and be committed to using the skill regularly. The program started with myself and one person on my team, Anthony Williamson. Anthony and I soon recruited a techie named Andrew from my reporting team who was interested. From there, a few others on the reporting team became interested, and we were soon on our way.

We found a use case related to smartphone device unlocking that was performed in the back office. No trade secrets, but there was a lot of manual work, usually too much for any team to handle without a backlog. I partnered with a couple leaders who managed that part of the business, Becky and Jason, and we finished 2018 with over 2 million transactions automated. We kept finding new use cases, often more complex as time went on, and we closed out 2019 eclipsing 8 million transactions automated. The following year was five times more, with over $40M in a variety of savings. I'm also very proud to say that through working with an array of leaders, we were able to reskill and repurpose employees instead of the alternative.

All that to say, with such a robust RPA program, I would have quarterly meetings with my RPA provider, Ramesh from Prodapt. At the time, what was top of mind for me was that we had a successful bot program doing amazing things in the back office. However, we hadn't quite cracked the code on automating things for frontline customer-facing employees.

So, when Ramesh and I met, I explained the dilemma. He shared a vendor with me that was doing some remarkable work for AT&T Mexico, the division of the company south of the border. This vendor is called CallVU/FICX. They're very small and based not far from our AT&T foundry in Tel Aviv. My first step was to meet with the VP of product, Daniel, a guy from New York who had relocated to Israel. Prior to his current role, Daniel had deployed a couple mobile music applications and had also spent years as an amateur boxer. So, in short, we're talking about an incredibly bright, driven guy who gets to the point.

During my initial discussions with Daniel in late 2018, we white-boarded how we could deploy something incredibly cutting edge called a Visual IVR (VIVR) in late 2019. An IVR is an Interactive Voice Response system. This is what you encounter when you call just about any customer service number that routes your call to the correct department. Over time, IVRs have evolved from Touchstone IVRs (press 1 for billing and 2 for support) to Speech Recognition IVRs (just talk to me in your normal language) to now a Visual IVR. This VIVR project carried at 3X in-year ROI, which constitutes as a strong business case. Specifically, a 300 percent return on investment means the return/benefit is triple the cost of the project. My team and I typically focus on projects and efforts, new ideas, and concepts that deliver a 5X, 10X, 20X ROI. However, because this project was so novel and progressive, I was a very strong supporter from the beginning.

Our project was approved and funded, but like most projects that start late in the fiscal year, we were delayed. As the year 2020 began, the issues delaying the project cleared, and we were approved to move forward. In a large company, it can take a while for the funding to route through the process, so it was mid-February by the time the project was just getting the wheels turning. Just as we were getting the project underway, the coronavirus was reaching pandemic-level impact. By mid-March, our project for Visual IVR was put on hold. No one knew what COVID-19 would mean for the future of the world, and, like many firms, we needed to assess what the new future might look like. Daniel and I were both disappointed, as we had worked on this effort for a long time and were excited about the new capabilities we were about to introduce to the American public.

Not to mention that 40,000 customer service employees can take about 800,000 calls a day. With payments as the most common call type and sales being one of the most critical/treasured, this was a huge issue, and, in some ways, health-wise, it was a matter of life or death.

Well, about a week after our project was put on hold, I reached out to Daniel from FICX to talk about the pandemic issue and any solutions we might be able to come up with together. Thankfully, Daniel had several tricks in his bag. One of his tricks was a collaboration tool that would allow an agent to send a web form to a customer. It was a great start, but it didn't address the FCC rules about not displaying SPI data to employees who were working from home.

And that's precisely when he and I began to ideate and innovate. After about an hour and a half, we conceptually figured out the masking and encryption half of the equation, but we still needed a way to import that info into our existing/legacy systems.

So, let's summarize.

- For four years, I had been pitching a revolutionary concept for working from home.
- Then, I met with a senior leader that didn't go quite as well as expected.
- But I had a small vendor with visual IVR capabilities.
- Enter March 2020: Visual IVR project is put on hold as the coronavirus was quickly reaching pandemic-level impact.
- Then, the United States government mandated shelter in place, and my four-year-old concept for working from home was displaced.

Of course, at this point, I had my character to stand on as well as my previous overcomer experiences.

- My sister, my hero, won the most miraculous battle against stage four cancer.
- I, myself, had survived near-death experiences.
- I came from the toughest corner of the city.
- My colleagues and their organizations were going through some pretty hefty challenges... and I never run from challenges.
- My boss trusted me.

My past problem-solving experiences—from Saint Anthony candy to Credit Decision Engines—had prepared me for this moment. Because of my passion and experience (especially the miracle faith-walk of my sister's victory), I knew I was not simply going to try but *would* accomplish doing something that had never been done before. I was going to ask some of the smartest folks in the industry to do some tremendously technical things that we hadn't done before with an accelerated timeline, during a critical time, and with a very unique funding source and support structure. But I knew that together, we were going to change how people think about work environments forever.

My past problem-solving experiences
—from Saint Anthony candy
to Credit Decision Engines—
had prepared me for this moment.

Winners Take Risks

I KNEW THERE WOULD BE SOME HURDLES in the process we were undertaking. Trying to deliver the solution fast, as well as working with a third-party vendor, would present some unique challenges. I was well aware that some important stakeholders might have had their own philosophy regarding new and unfamiliar concepts. So, the first thing I did was connect with some friends who owned or managed the actual application in which we needed to make some enhancements.

The folks I connected with that managed the actual applications were also friends of mine. They were people I knew from previous projects or people who knew of my previous high-ROI projects. They are rock stars in their field and were all-in on solving the next big issue for our customers and the general public, and the pandemic-level predicament between the FCC rules and shelter in place was it.

Every crisis is in need of a solution, and people are searching for a hero. Superheroes need mountains to move. They need challenges that will challenge them. Small stuff won't hold their attention for long. These friends were superheroes.

Every crisis is in need of a solution,
and people are searching for a hero.

One of the first friends I started to work with to technically solve the issue and take it from actual white-boarding to wrench-turning was Prasada Pudi, commonly known to many as Pudi. Pudi is a consummate professional. He knows his area of focus like the back of his hand, but there is one thing that makes Pudi a little different. He is a winner through and through, and he's not afraid to bet on himself. And, if you haven't gathered it by now: neither am I.

During our first conversation, I explained how the FICX collaboration tool with modifications could solve this FCC/SPI data issue. Pudi understood the work-from-home dilemma and why I was leveraging this collaboration capability to create this secure experience. So, we had the solution for retrieving the data from the customer, encrypting the entire experience, and masking the sensitive customer information from the agent. But we still needed a way to import that information back into the legacy/existing systems.

Oh, and "quickly" does not fully encapsulate the true urgency and expediency in which we needed to complete the effort.

Pudi mentioned that there was an API that was created (but not in use) to do something *similar* but not quite the same. An API is an Application Programming Interface. In simple terms, APIs are backdoors to different information or capabilities of a system. For example, I could build a bot to manually mimic what a person would do, as in step 1, step 2, step 3, and so on. However, an API would skip past the manual steps to navigate through a system and get to the task completion nearly instantly. Pudi had an API that could handle the second half of the solution (sending payments into our internal system). However, this API was not in use. It was just sitting on the shelf. And it was most certainly not guaranteed to be a feasible reuse option.

The API that Pudi referenced enabled a slingshot-like capability. If you're familiar with APIs, it might already sound like this was easy. Just repurpose one API for another. However, APIs don't always work that way.

APIs are often written with very specific instructions to accomplish very specific tasks. Some are able to accomplish multiple tasks, while some APIs can only perform one task. Either way, APIs are typically designed with these detailed instructions so they do the exact thing they are intended to do—very fast and without failure.

When you're talking about an API written to accomplish a task for an external partner, it will have some interface with an internal system. However, an API like that is going to be written with boundaries to ensure nothing goes awry. Pudi believed that if we were flexible and determined, then we could make enough modifications within the FICX application to actually repurpose this API and successfully slingshot the encrypted, masked, SPI data into the internal system. Technically, this was going to be like Robin Hood shooting an arrow into another arrow that's stuck in a tree. Difficult even for a superhero and not guaranteed to work. But again, Pudi is a winner. Once we had the technical feasibility identified, I knew what the next step would be.

I called my VP, Trish Renz, and shared the entire vision with her. I explicitly asked her for her engagement in the effort because I knew that we would need a lot of escalations to accomplish the feat expeditiously. Trish, being the true visionary that she is, was 100 percent supportive and asked me what I needed. I asked her for an angel—a subject matter expert in the area I knew I was going to have to forge a warp-speed path forward. She sent us to a proven leader, David Brickhaus, VP, who then introduced us to Brad Greenwell, one of his top project managers. However, I needed one more angel. Before I could even ask, Sherish Hedden called me.

Sherish was the director over consumer operations (remember, I worked on the business side) and would typically be the person to lead something like this for the consumer call center organization. Sherish and I were friends long before this situation arose, and we had worked on some smaller initiatives to improve the experience in our retail stores. Sherish is smart and well-respected. She put in the hard work and really understood how all the pieces worked together and the politics that are sometimes present. She heard what we were working on in the business organization and shared that her side of the company was going through the same dilemma and wanted to know if we could partner together on a solution.

I'm always looking to find a "yes," and I happily told her, "Sure, let's do it."

I'm always looking to find a "yes."

I firmly believe teamwork makes the dream work, and Sherish lives this. She understands the big picture and is not territorial. She truly believes we win together. Sherish is an angel that connected me with another critical angel I needed, an angel from the Corporate Security Organization (CSO). The angel Sherish connected me with on the CSO side was the well-respected Signe Jackson. With Brad at my right hand, CSO on my left, and Trish supporting every step, we had a great start.

Sherish and I partnered on co-funding the effort from the business and consumer organizations. Typically, there is a very clear separation regarding the development and funding of efforts between business and consumer. However, Brad blazed through doors like Neo in "The Matrix". Signe cleared more red tape in less time than I've seen in my entire career. As you can imagine, the company is very particular about who, what, and what level of access is permitted through our firewalls and/ or traversing our network. With Signe, we checked every box. The load-balancing effort to not only develop something that can be used but to *fortify* the solution so 40,000 colleagues around the world could use the functionality simultaneously without latency/failure is hard to wrap your mind around.

Friends like Henry Do, Glen Johnstone, Kiran Komallpalli, Jacqueline McPaul, Raja Amble, Lisa Saunders, Dennis Winkeler, Milin Patel, and Vasanth Kumar Murali are truly Justice League-level professionals. This effort would not have finished successfully without them. Period. Again, superheroes need super challenges. During these extreme crunch times is when they get to fully show their superpowers.

Every aspect of what it takes to accomplish something like this had to be designed, executed, documented, tested, and deployed. We asked a lot of teams to do things that they had never done before, and to do them much faster than normal. This can cause some friction. Even when people have the best of intentions, if the stakes and stress are high, the wrong tone can cause the dynamics of a project to turn unproductive.

Going in knowing this, I did something that had not been done before. When using our web conferencing, I changed my name from "David C. Williams" to "Optimis'tic Prime." It was something to have a little fun and strategically set the tone. We needed everyone to remain optimistic for all the right reasons: for the success of the project, for the employees we would enable, for the customers needing those employees' support, for the balance of positivity against all that was going wrong in the world at the time, and for the sake of getting a job done that no other group of people were skilled and in position to accomplish.

Destiny was calling, and it was our time. Day in and day out, I would do my best to weave a little fun into every call, whether using funny Southern analogies, creative metaphors, or one-liners. I was determined to ensure that the tone of every meeting was optimistic. Even if we hit a roadblock, we would not lose confidence in ourselves to overcome whatever challenge was before us. I openly referred to the members of the team as *superheroes* and proactively spoke to people's strengths and their importance to the team in front of their peers. For example, if we had to detour from technically building to having a meeting with our legal team to explain how what we were doing was compliant from one perspective or another, then somewhere at the beginning of that discussion, I would say something like:

> "We're happy to explain this for you. I'll provide an overview, and then I'd like Henry Do to take you through step-by-step so you can see exactly how we cared for that. Henry helped design this solution from the ground up. He's the best in the business, and we are in the best hands possible. Not only will this work, but it's going to *securely* work globally and without any customer impact in the event of an issue."

At that point, Henry, who truly is one of the brightest minds when it comes to his area of focus, Network Topology and Load Balancing, had a captive audience waiting on the edge of their seats to see and hear him do the thing he was passionate and perfectly positioned to do. In addition to that, every other superhero on this project team could see for themselves that they would be recognized during *and* after the project.

I also want to mention that some of our cross-functional team was suffering from the impacts of COVID-19. Some had family members who were impacted. Some of us had colleagues who tested positive. Thankfully, none of the folks on our core team contracted the virus. But when your heroes hurt, when their close ones hurt, you hurt. My mother and niece were both diagnosed with COVID-19 in early May and quarantined over Mother's Day. My mom was 75 years young. She is my inspiration and has been an amazing role model of a person—a woman, a leader, a parent. I couldn't ask for more in a parent.

At the very end of the project, someone who outranked me threw a last-minute option on the table. They stated that they could build a similar solution—all internally—within a couple of weeks. Well, we didn't have two more weeks to wait. We couldn't afford any additional delays. So, do you go with a bird in the hand or two in the bush?

The decision was made to go with the solution that was already created and wait no longer. The contracts were signed and finalized, and we were off to the races.

The reps loved the solution we deployed. It did everything we needed it to do. No more having to put customers on hold while desperately trying to reach someone in the call centers. No more referring customers online because of missing capabilities. The pressure was relieved, and work-from-home customer service operations in the telecommunications world had begun.

Bring Your Best

FOLLOWING THIS ACCOMPLISHMENT, my vice president, Trish Renz, nominated me for a BEYA STEM (Black Engineer of the Year Award-Science Technology Education Math) award. The first letters of recommendation came from the incomparable Anne Chow, CEO of AT&T Business, who wrote a two-page letter of recommendation along with our leader John Stankey, CEO of AT&T Inc. The next was from Mo Katibeh, our chief platform/product officer (and also the sponsor of that 23xROI-CDE-project). Additional letters of recommendation were written by David Huntley, chief compliance officer and Xavier Williams, president. Additionally, Vedant Jhavar, CEO of Prodapt (the sky is the limit, my friend) and Michael Oiknine, CEO of CallVU/FICX (what can't we do together) also wrote, of recommendation on my behalf for the BEYA award. The last letter of recommendation I received was from my brother, Kenneth Gwyn. The greatest man I know is Kenneth.

The results were in, and I received a call from the selection committee. I was the recipient of the Rodney Adkins Legacy Award at the 2021 BEYA STEM Global Competitiveness Conference. Normally, I'm a private guy, but a really good friend of mine, Shaun Harris, posted the announcement on Twitter. That post received tens of thousands of views per week, and that started a lot more.

Due to COVID, the awards were held virtually. Anne Chow presented the award to me with a warm and heartfelt introduction. The following is my acceptance speech—a microcosm displaying my past experiences combined with my professional passion that led me to a unique business model of success.

You are one of one. There will never be anyone like you. And as the world moves faster, the sound bites get shorter, the less we pay attention, the more we categorize (which is a slippery slope to stereotyping and next-door neighbors to prejudging each other), remember: you are one of one. You are not supposed to act just like, talk just like, walk just like *anyone*. Everyone may not fully appreciate your math or formula, even if they ultimately benefit from the result.

The math was meant for you.

You are one of one.
There will never be anyone like you.

My math? Simple. I bring my best self; you bring your best self, and let's do something exponential together because I believe that one and one is 11. And "four divided by two minus one equals one, which means you really cannot lose if you've already won," said my mother, Alice Williams.

Thank you, God.

Conclusion

AS WE COME TO THE END OF THIS BOOK, I want to remind you of a few things in closing that I hope have been illustrated by my challenges in life, my victories—and, ultimately, my story.

You are a business model. Period. Your experiences, combined with your passion, create your unique business model. Leverage it. Do not shy away from it. Remember Rudolph, the Red-Nosed Reindeer. If that's too fictional for you, consider the fact that many of the most extraordinarily famous or wildly successful people did not start off that way. Often, they were laughed at, ridiculed, or cast out. They came from humble beginnings. Of the CEOs I mentioned earlier, one received their degree through the company's tuition aid program. Another lived in a home with 11 people. I've been able to witness powerful, world-shaping individuals who overcame some tough challenges by fully leveraging their experiences, immersing themselves in their professional passion, and igniting their own means of doing business—*their* business model.

Every human has the potential to make their mark on the world. Every human. I'm making my mark on the world. Not for money or fame, but for the progress of advancing technology and inspiring others. The greatest gift one person can give another is the gift of inspiration. I'm grateful for the opportunity to show others whose experiences may have been similar to my own—or completely different—that the best things in life are within reach.

Your life experiences give you a competitive advantage. Leverage that advantage. Remember, you don't have a chance if you don't take one. No matter your situation, whether you come from suburban communities and have your own unique obstacles to overcome or if, like me, you come from inner-city under-served communities, the following truth stands: the things you have learned to get this far in life are usually transferable skills that you most certainly should *not* leave in the parking lot before you go to work.

Your life experiences give you
a competitive advantage.

A great friend of mine, Geno, often says, "In the game of life, you only need one home run. So keep swinging." Start now. You gotta start taking steps so they can turn into strides. You will not make it out of this life alive, so you must live it to the fullest. But often, you don't know if you are walking/living/working as your best until you push the limit to some degree. What are you waiting for? You, your aspirations, and your dreams are not a risk. They are within reach if you are courageously willing to make the journey. They are your goals, and I believe that all respectful dreams of goodwill are achievable.

If you look back across your own life, you will see evidence of triumph in the darkest times of your journey. In fact, if you're reading this book, then you have survived the worst health crisis of our generation. Your time is now. You've already lived the past. You have the experience(s). You've had a glimpse of what is possible. The only component missing is the passion to pursue those dreams beyond any logic or failure.

Now, you will need more passion than there is fear. Some of the closest people to you might even *provide* the fear. They may think you are reaching too far. They might lovingly be afraid of you failing and being disappointed. They may be afraid that if you level up, you won't want or need them. They may fear your success will be their demise. Thinking like this is just people acting out of desperation or self-preservation. Do not ignore their projections, rather, become conscious that they are choosing not to participate in what it takes to reach your goal. That's their choice, not yours. It's okay. They may come around later; who knows. Don't put energy into it. Don't fall into any negativity. Simply accept the facts and act on faith. Remember, the greatest prison is the one people put themselves into by worrying what others think of them.

Your story will usually surprise you with more greatness than you could have imagined if you allow room to master the art of the possible. More often than not, we have more power than we have the guts to use. I've found that the innovative, creative, and unique characteristics to propel you to rise to the occasion are already *within* you. An apple seed comes with the master plan to create an entire orchard of apple trees: roots, leaves, tree trunk, bark, and fruit color are all included. All that seed needs is a chance to grow to its *full* potential.

Will you give yourself a chance?

About the Author

DAVID C. WILLIAMS, Assistant Vice President, Automation Robotics Process Automation/Emerging Tech, AT&T Business Solutions. In these roles David has created deep-link HTML marketing initiatives that garner 90 million monthly impressions, has led Competitive Intelligence which helped shape AT&T's Mobile First strategy and employee discounts, has been responsible for supporting several Fortune 500 companies encompassing $120 million in revenue, and authored two patents for Reprogrammable RFID and bridging satellite and LTE technology.

In his current role, David is responsible for hyper-automation & emerging technology to transform Customer/Employee Experience and Cost Structure for his organization. He leads the largest Robotics Process Automation program worldwide. His innovations are driving change across the company as his team has developed 600+ bots automating 70,000 contacts, realizing $400 million in operating income at over 3,000 percent ROI. Additionally, he also invented and sponsored a machine-learning decision engine driving $200M credit reduction annually.

David is also working to deploy his own cryptocurrency, the Anomaly token. And he enjoys family activities, volunteering, fitness training, and motorcycle riding.